CLASSROOM CIRCLES

DR. Tim B. Smart

CLASSROOM CIRCLES

A Toolkit for Building Relationships and Strengthening School Communities

JOHN J. WHALEN

With Contributions from
Denise "Circle Mamma" Holliday-Jones
Foreword by Kevin W. Curtis

© 2018 ED311
All Rights Reserved

No part of this book may be reproduced without the express consent of ED311

512 W. Martin Luther King Jr. Blvd., #300
Austin, TX 78701
512-478-2113
info@ed311.com
www.ed311.com

First Printing: December 2018
Second Printing: March 2019
Third Printing: September 2019

ISBN 978-1-947753-06-8

Contents

Acknowledgments	vii
Foreword by Kevin W. Curtis	xi
About NEDRP	xiii

PART I
The Ins and Outs of Circles

1.	Introduction: How I Found Circle Circle Mamma's Diary #1: What I Needed from a Teacher	3
2.	The 5 Ws of Circle and the Evolution of Classroom Circles Circle Mamma's Diary #2: Courage and Bravery	16
3.	The Facilitator Mind-Set Circle Mamma's Diary #3: They Say Circle Doesn't Work for Those Kids	26
4.	The Physical Circle Circle Mamma's Diary #4: Creating a Positive Environment	35
5.	The Components of Circle Circle Mamma's Diary #5: The Power of Values	44
6.	The Flexibility of Circles: Green, Yellow, Red Circle Mamma's Diary #6: Let Circle Take Its Course	59

7. Tips and Strategies for Facilitating Circle   78
   Circle Mamma's Diary #7: My Why—Healing Hearts,
   One Circle at a Time

PART II
Circle Scripts   95

PART III
Circle Building Tools   119

References   137

Acknowledgments

John J. Whalen

First and foremost, I want to thank my family. To my wife, Cortney, thank you for letting me put so many hours into something that I am so passionate about. I'm amazed at how seamlessly you can carry the family on your back when I'm running around the country, staying late at work, or sitting in a coffee shop working on a seemingly never-ending book. Thank you for always standing by me, even in times when I have been difficult. To my two daughters, Moira and Emma Jo, I love both of you much more than infinity. I'm continually in awe of how kind and compassionate both of you are.

To my parents, John and Mary Ellen Whalen, thank you for giving me a wonderful example to follow. I'm grateful that I was lucky enough to have two such amazing parents. Thank you for pushing me to further my education and sustaining me along the way. To my siblings, Kerry and Patrick, thank you for your continuing interest in what I do. To my in-laws, Rick and Jackie, thank you for all of your help and support.

To the Binghamton City School District (BCSD)—#BPatriotProud—many thanks for supporting Restorative Practices. I will be forever grateful that the district has given me so many opportunities to grow both professionally and personally.

To my colleagues over the last 17 years of working in the BCSD, thank you for your leadership, advice, guidance, and especially the laughter that I have experienced in our work together. I particularly want to thank our superintendent, Dr. Tonia Thompson, for believing in me. I also want to thank my Bloc 600 team at East Middle School: Alicia, Jack, Keith, Kelly, Becky, Kerry, and Jason. Each of you helped me grow as a teacher and made the workplace a fun place to be!

To the students of the Binghamton City School District, thank you for teaching me more about life than you could ever imagine. I'm truly blessed to have worked with such amazing young people.

ACKOWLEDGMENTS

To my good friend Kevin Curtis, thank you for inviting me to come along on this restorative journey. Your passion for the work we do is unmatched. I'm so glad that our paths crossed years ago. Thank you for believing in me and for always being willing to listen.

To my other colleagues at National Educators for Restorative Practices (NEDRP), thank you for all that you have taught me, shared with me, and experienced with me as we have participated in this incredible adventure.

To everyone at Park Place Publications, thank you for helping this idea become a reality.

Acknowledgments

Denise "Circle Mamma" Holliday-Jones

Reflecting on this journey and the people who have enabled and equipped me to take it has been its own blessing. Maybe thanking the whole world isn't a bad way to begin.

First and foremost, I would like to give honor to God, for without Him none of this would be possible.

To my kids—Kameron Holliday, Avery Holliday, and Bruce Jones, Jr.—Mommy thanks all of you for your unconditional love and support. Kameron, I'm so grateful you've chosen to share your restorative journey by my side. I hope that other young people may find their voice just as you found yours. Avery, thank you especially for reminding me that there must be balance in this process.

To my husband, Bruce, I express my gratitude for your support and your constant prayers of traveling grace.

To my mother, Nevada Cyphers, thanks for always believing in me and being my biggest cheerleader, even amid trials and tribulations. I thank you for encouraging me and for being an excellent example of a strong woman.

To my brothers, Len and Derrick, it truly warms my heart to look into your eyes and know that I make you both proud. No other words needed.

To my dad, Homer Cyphers, and my stepmother, Christine Cyphers, thank you both for prayers of support and constantly checking on me. I can always count on that call from you asking, "Where are you today?"

To Dr. Marcus Jones, you saw my vision and fostered my growth. Thank you, Dr. Jones, for opening the curtain to my stage.

To Life Anew, for introducing me to my restorative life, and Eric Butler, whose passion and presence inspired me and lit a spark within me that will last forever.

To Dr. Marilyn Armour and the Institute for Restorative Justice and Restorative Dialogue at the University of Texas at Austin, a special thanks for believing in me and allowing me to let my light shine. I will never forget the words you spoke in your office: "You have something I can't teach to anyone." I often remember those words at challenging moments.

To Kevin Curtis, you saw my value even when I did not. You always had a way of pulling me out of the shadows of others so that I could see my worth. I'm so grateful for your encouragement and for introducing me to who "Circle Mamma" is. You are truly a blessing.

To my mentor, my sister Kris Miner Schwieger, thank you for always being there to hold my hand and lift my head when I need it. I especially thank you for helping me to genuinely grasp the spirit of this work.

And finally, to my NEDRP family, thank you for lifting me up.

Foreword

Kevin W. Curtis

This book will not only educate you but will undoubtedly inspire you as well. John Whalen has taken every ounce of the passion that he has developed throughout his many years in education and poured his heart, mind, and soul into this project. I am extremely proud of how John has devoted that passion to the concepts of Restorative Practices, enthusiastically subscribing to the NEDRP belief that as educators we must share information and ideas in a way that is meaningful and practical for all teachers at all levels.

When I first met John, he was a wide-eyed teacher from Binghamton (New York) City Schools visiting our middle school campus in San Antonio, Texas. Our school, Ed White Middle School, in the Northeast Independent School District, was attempting to be the first in the state of Texas to implement a school-wide approach to learning called Restorative Practices, which featured classroom circles as a strategy to achieve its goals. During John's visit, you could see his inquisitive nature at work as he wrestled with how to make circles a reality in his own classrooms at East Middle School.

Not only did John take his experiences from Texas back to upstate New York, but he quickly developed his own style of circles in the classroom. After fully training John and his staff members at East Middle School, I returned to their campus every other month to observe, coach, and support. Each and every time I visited his classroom, I was impressed with the progress that John was making in honing his craft. John's thought processes work very differently from the way mine do, and our shared passion for developing solutions to make classroom circles more practical and "teacher-friendly" drove both of us to create unique approaches to the typical classroom circle.

What John presents in this book is a culmination of the ideas and experiences of many collaborators, but he has taken the time to put our insights and words into an easy format that will allow educators to relate to and benefit from his accumulated wisdom. Whether you are an educator who is already adept at conducting circles in your classroom or a novice anticipating your first encounters with circles, this book will meet your needs.

One of the most powerful portions of the material included in this volume is the collection of Denise Holliday-Jones's "Circle Mamma's Diary" entries, which appear between chapters. Recognizing that Denise, known as "Circle Mamma," has been anointed with a special gift when it comes to facilitating circles in any type of setting, John incorporated these pieces as an invaluable and unique way of offering more tools for learning about circles.

John Whalen is more than a colleague to me. He has become a friend and a brother. I thank God that my life has intersected with those of John and his family, school family, and friends. The value they bring to the work continues to shape the ministry that is National Educators for Restorative Practices.

About NEDRP

Educators across the country increasingly face student behaviors in the classroom that interfere with the learning process and result in the loss of valuable instructional time. In the current culture of high-stakes testing and accountability, the pressure to demonstrate student achievement weighs more heavily than ever before. Classroom teachers are becoming more and more frustrated with persistent misbehavior and frequently resort to exclusionary practices or referrals to school administration. Administrators, in turn, are limited to the same few "cookie cutter" approaches to managing student behavior that stopped being effective for most of them years ago. Relationships between teachers and students and between teachers and administrators are suffering. Out of options and up against zero-tolerance policies and inflexible adult mind-sets, administrators nationwide are searching for strategies that will allow them to address "the root" of challenging student behaviors rather than simply "treating the fruit." The cycle is difficult to break, but it must be proactively addressed in order to ensure that educators and students gain the opportunity to teach and to learn within an inclusive community.

National Educators for Restorative Practices (NEDRP) is committed to becoming the unifying voice for all educators by providing leadership, guidance, and resources for the implementation of the Restorative Practices approach, with the goal of helping schools meet the educational needs of all students. NEDRP is an organization that aims to bring educators the tools necessary to utilize the Restorative Practices approach with authenticity. The NEDRP model, "By Educators for Educators," focuses on using real-world classroom and campus applications through professional development, certifications, and consulting. We exist to create experiences during which passion and purpose combine to help change relationships on a campus *one educator at a time*.

ABOUT NEDRP

In 2015, Kevin Curtis started Restorative Discipline 360 (RD360), presenting to administrators throughout the state of Texas the concepts of Restorative Practices and what he had discovered while introducing that model as an assistant principal at Ed White Middle School in San Antonio, the first campus in the entire state of Texas to undertake a full school implementation. He learned what worked and what didn't, then drew upon his experiences to begin developing the model that NEDRP uses today.

In 2016, Kevin changed the original name, Restorative Discipline 360, to Texas Educators for Restorative Practices (TEXRP) and brought a few more people on board, including Denise Holliday-Jones and John Whalen, to help meet the needs of the organization's increasingly busy schedule. During the summer of 2016, the small staff worked mostly in the state of Texas, training more than 1,000 educators and administrators with the "By Educators for Educators" model of Restorative Practices. The rapid growth continued, and by the summer of 2017, four lead trainers, working in four states, reached an estimated 3,000 teachers. The move beyond the borders of Texas prompted another name change, this time to National Educators for Restorative Practices (NEDRP). Plans for summer 2018 involved trainings in a total of six states.

NEDRP training programs are just as much experiences as they are learning sessions. Participants have their usual expectations challenged over the course of the one-, two-, and three-day events. Teachers, administrators, social workers, counselors, parents, and community members not only *learn* about the power of Restorative Practices, they *experience* the power. The overwhelmingly positive feedback from attendees inspires the staff to work even harder to meet the needs of those who participate in the training. Here is a selection of responses to a three-day training conducted with school administrators and teacher leaders:

"Keep doing what you're doing. Definitely a fantastic process and training."

"The training was fun, interactive, and informative. The material was made easy to digest because of the layers and practice. Love the positive and energetic atmosphere."

"The training was phenomenal! I came to the training thinking I'd be getting some really good strategies, but I gained so much more. I have built relationships and grown spiritually. Thank you, thank you, and thank you."

"I have attended many different trainings over my career, and this is in the top three (and actually #1). This approach from educators and presented by

About NEDRP

educators has so much more meaning to me. Now that I have been exposed to Restorative Practices, I am excited to bring this model to my staff and my students. My only complaint is that I didn't have this earlier to share with some of my 'babies' that I could have maybe reached a little better. Thank you so much for teaching me, keeping me in the GREEN, and helping my heart grow a little bigger. You are all angels and ROCKSTARS!! I will see you again!"

"One of the best three-day trainings I've ever been to! I would love for NEDRP to infiltrate my school and our entire district. I can't wait to share with everyone all of the vital information covered in this training. Thank you for being so raw and telling it like it is in schools. Keep doing what you're doing, guys—your ministry is changing lives!"

"Wow! Such a meaningful learning experience! Throughout the last two years, I have attended several Restorative Practices trainings. However, I must say that this is the most informative, energy-filled RP session that I ever attended. Kevin [Curtis] coached us in a way that showed us how we would be able to relate this information to our current situations on our individual campuses/districts, and gave us examples of ways to implement these practices no matter where we are on this journey. That's amazing! Kudos to [Kevin] and [his] team for asking us throughout the sessions if our individual expectations/needs were being met in order to make sure we were getting the most out of the training. The team was approachable, full of heart, and resourceful. Keep doing the "good work" of changing how educators work with students one training at a time. I will be attending the conference in October, and I plan to bring an army of others with me! Thank you."

These comments encompass the feelings and dedication of the NEDRP team. We truly love the work that we do and the power of the message we offer. Transformation can begin to happen when the practices we share are brought to a campus with authenticity and a shared vision of all stakeholders.

Please contact me at johnjwhalen@nedrp.com if you are interested in learning more about what NEDRP does with school districts and individual schools. Other services are available for higher education, teacher preparation programs, and the workforce. And finally, please do not hesitate to reach out with questions, ideas, or stories about circles!

PART I

The Ins and Outs of Circles

CHAPTER 1

Introduction: How I Found Circle

> The greatest discovery of all time is that a person can change his future by merely changing his attitude.
>
> —Oprah Winfrey

Finding Circle: My Experience

Middle school (aka sixth grade) can be a wild place. You have to be a little crazy to work in a building filled with more than 550 adolescents who roam the halls searching for meaning in the ever-changing world opening up before them. Some classes sit quietly and follow the lead of the teacher. These are the classes that we all imagined while studying for our undergraduate teaching degrees. Most classes would be like this (or so we thought). Other classes make us laugh as we get caught up in the exciting waves that a connected group of individuals can create in an ocean of respect and understanding. Some of our classes, though, make us earn that paycheck. The students may not be interested in what we're teaching (or buying what we're selling, as I usually put it) and may not be all that interested in us. Veteran teachers can usually navigate these waters by creating dynamic lessons that are interesting and relevant to the students. They can use top-shelf tools like collaborative learning, games, technology, and humor. During the 12 years that I spent teaching sixth-grade mathematics, I experienced all of this. The lesson planning, the great classes, the ones that made me sweat, and the ways I figured out how to keep those classes moving along regardless. And then, a few years ago, along came *that* sixth-period class.

I knew by the end of the second week of school that it would be the most challenging class I had ever had. I spent those those first weeks pleading for student attention, playing the shell game with my seating chart, intervening in student conflicts, and watching lesson after lesson fail. I told myself, "I'll figure this out. I've been doing this for a while, and this group won't break me. If they try to break me, I'll just bring back Camp Whalen."

Camp Whalen, created on a whim one frustrating day during my early years of teaching, was a place that would not score high on a middle schooler's rating list. However, it was an authoritarian's dream. My voice is loud and it sure can carry. No one was going to talk over me. I would simply turn up the volume higher than the students did. I'd teach louder. Disrespect would not be tolerated and would often be countered by a sarcastic comment from yours truly. Violation of any of the rules or regulations of Camp Whalen called for an instant consequence that was non-negotiable. If a student expressed displeasure with my judgment, I would simply make the consequence more severe. And more severe. And more severe yet. I think you get the point of Camp Whalen. Anyway, my thought was that through my use of such tactics, this class would eventually conform to my expectations. I knew it wouldn't happen overnight, so I prepared for a marathon. Maybe I'd have the class fine-tuned by Halloween.

Halloween came and went. The class had actually begun to act *worse*. Nothing was working. Half of the students made it close to impossible for the rest of them to concentrate, let alone learn anything. My first strategy was to move some of the successful students out of this class and into one of my other classes, where they could learn. I had a few students leave the school for other campuses. By the middle of November, I had a class of 13 students during this period. Roughly 10 of them had not responded to a single intervention or change that I had implemented throughout the year. Consequently the issues had not been resolved. I was lost. I would come to school with dread in the pit of my stomach each day, wondering how I would be able to get through sixth period.

Then I was asked to be part of a district committee that would look at district discipline statistics and brainstorm solutions for the alarming discipline issues at our school. Our district superintendent approached me about going to a two-day workshop on Restorative Justice. I had heard of Restorative Justice a few months earlier and brought it to the attention of the district committee and administrators. I was quick to jump at the opportunity. I did have a bit of anxiety about it, though. How on earth could I leave this sixth-period class with a substitute for two days? Luckily, our grade-level consultant teacher volunteered to help out, and that alleviated my anxiety. And two days without that dread in my stomach? Sign me up!

The workshop was fantastic. It covered elements of Restorative Justice ranging from the judicial system to the education system. We heard presentations from academics, attorneys, released felons, and victims of

Introduction: How I Found Circle

violent crime. They kept talking about something called a "circle process" that was used to guide the conversation to repair harm between two or more parties. I strolled through the lobby of the university building that hosted the conference and went to the merchandise table. There I found a book about group circles, which I quickly purchased, since it was the last one. I hoped this book would help me to understand circles and learn how I could use them to facilitate change between parties who were in conflict.

I started reading the book as I rode along with our assistant principal during the three-hour trip home. I soon found out that the book I'd bought really had nothing to do with the types of circles I had heard about at the conference. Just my luck! Nevertheless, I continued to read and learned about group meetings that were called circles. They followed a specific process that was intended to bring communities of people together. I began to think of my sixth-period class. Did I dare try one of these circles with them? I felt that there was nothing to lose. As things now stood, I was lucky to get 15 minutes of quality instruction in with this group. I remembered what I had read in Eric Jensen's book *Teaching with Poverty in Mind*: "No curriculum, instruction, or assessment, however high-quality, will succeed in a hostile social climate" (Jensen 2009, 87). Maybe I would try these circles for the next week and see where they would take us. I had the book that I had just bought that contained some circle themes. I could just follow the script and see what happened. This would be the first thing that I would do with my sixth-period class when I returned on Monday.

On Monday the students walked in and immediately got perplexed looks on their faces. The desks were arranged in a circle in the middle of the classroom. The students came in with the same noisiness and lack of respect that I usually encountered. I had a basketball in my hand as I sat down (I was working lunch, and I had been playing with a group of students). I grabbed the book, opened it at random to the page of a scripted circle, and swallowed deeply. "Here goes nothing," I thought. I had to wait a minute or two for the class to settle down. They eventually did, but I think it was out of curiosity about what I was doing. I told them about my trip to the conference and showed them on the map of New York State where I had been.

"You probably are wondering a few things," I said. "We are sitting in a class circle. We've struggled as a class this year. You guys have struggled. I have struggled. I feel that we should try this with the hope of building a better classroom. This circle has nothing to do with math. It's about getting to know one another better. I plan on doing these every day for the next week. Are you guys good with this?" The students looked around at one another. I could see the shoulders shrugging and the eyes rolling. Then this one student, the student who could never sit still, always shouted out, and would stoke the fire of any classroom conflict, yelled, "That means we don't have to do math this week?" I confirmed this. I still had the basketball in my hand. "This basketball is the talking piece. If you have it, you can talk. If you don't have it, you don't talk. Everyone got it?" Students yelled out things like "Yeah," "Yes," "Whatever." I glanced down at the script and started with the opener. The students looked at me strangely as I read an ancient quote to them. This was the opening of circle. I asked them if they could tell me what the quote meant. I passed the basketball to the student on my left. He looked at me and said nothing. He then sent a whizzing chest pass across to a student on the other side of the circle. This student responded with an immature remark that got the whole class laughing and yelling. "This was a fantastic idea, John," I thought to myself. The class was wilder now than it might ever have been. I grabbed the basketball and began to lecture the class on how disappointed I was in them. Do you think that worked?

That first day of circle was a total disaster. We got through only two of the questions I had planned. I don't think anyone took it seriously. Still, I was not going to give up. The next day they showed up and there it was: the circle. It took me a few days. It took patience. It took listening to my students complain about the idea. After maybe the fourth day I asked them, "If you could change one thing in your life, right now, what would it be?" I was expecting an immature answer about having boatloads of money, all the girls in the world, or something equally outrageous. But that's not what happened. Instead, the first student to answer just looked at the class and told everyone about how his aunt was raising him. He spoke about how his mother was not fit to raise him and said that he had been with his aunt for years. He spoke slowly but confidently about how he wished he could live with his mom again but knew that she wasn't well enough to take care of him. He then passed the talking piece to the person next to him (smartly, I had moved on from the idea of a basketball to using a stuffed animal and a bamboo stick). The class just sat there, stunned. His words hit me like a punch to the gut. I had never experienced anything like this in my classroom. Never had a student opened up to a whole class about something so personal. And now it was happening in my most difficult class ever. The next student sat there with the talking piece and began to talk about the difficulties that he encountered in moving to this country and not knowing the language. One by one, the students shared their deepest concerns. By the time the talking piece had been passed around the circle, almost everyone had shared.

The talking piece came back to me, and I remember pausing. I looked at the group differently after that one question—the question of what one thing they would change in their lives if they could change anything—had been answered. I thanked them for feeling comfortable enough to share with me

Introduction: How I Found Circle

and the group. After the circle ended that day, a subtle shift began that lasted throughout the remainder of the year. We met in circle each day for the rest of that week, and each day the circle grew stronger. When the students came in the next week, the desks were set in rows again. They protested that we were not in circle and pleaded that we put the circle back. We continued to meet in circle as a class almost every day, for the remainder of the year (after all, we did have to cover some math).

The students responded remarkably to the implementation of circle in our classroom. Around February or March, it got to the point that we could basically cover the content that the other classes were doing and still have between four and eight minutes left for circle. We kept the seats arranged in a circle, and we conducted our lessons in circle, sometimes using the talking piece to talk about the content. The class wasn't absolutely perfect, and there were days when an argument or disruption would occur. If that happened, we would stop what we were doing and return to circling. It was a much more productive and effective way to deal with conflict than the old Camp Whalen ways of doing things had been.

"Finding circle" was one of the key moments in my career. I realized that I had stumbled upon something that could be a powerful tool. I had to intentionally create opportunities to connect with my students. I had to connect with them at times other than those when conflicts came up. Relationships and rapport were key. As my friend Kevin Curtis put it so clearly, you have to **CONNECT** before you try to teach **CONTENT**! And for many struggling students, you have to **CONNECT** before you try to **CORRECT** their behavior. These insights led to my journey of promoting the philosophy of Restorative Practices at the school where I worked. They also became the impetus for me to learn how to serve as a facilitator. I was figuring out how to facilitate, but it wasn't until I met a lady named Denise that I really experienced and understood what circle is all about and what power it holds. Read on and you too will soon meet Denise.

Finding Circle: Doug Overton's Experience

I had the opportunity to meet and work with Doug during a training that we facilitated in 2017. Doug had been named Teacher of the Year for his district. He associates Restorative Practices—specifically relationship building circles—with his success. Below is his account of how circles have affected both him and his students.

No two days are ever the same for a P.E. teacher at the district's Alternative Learning Center. I could start with the day I had full participation in a game of football that ended with one of my female students outjumping two of the males to catch the winning touchdown pass. (Yes, I still teach competition; I believe it is vital for my kids in this environment.) I could write about a middle school volleyball lesson when my students broke the Learning Center's consecutive-hits record. I'll never forget the joy on their faces as they bounded around in triumph! But even for the Teacher of the Year, there are days when nothing goes right. I distinctly remember when I proposed a kickball game to my high school students and the entire class refused to participate. But games and sports aren't what define me as a teacher. What I really want to share are the lessons I teach on life, hope, and respect.

The Learning Center decided in spring 2016 to take a new approach to discipline, and the results in my classroom have been unbelievable. This new campus initiative, known as Restorative Practices, has transformed my classroom and given my kids a whole new outlook on life. Restorative Practices and, more importantly, relationship building circles, help students find an identity and give them the opportunity to receive positive encouragement. Every class period starts with circle. It's in circle that students become acclimated to their learning environment and get to know their peers and teacher from a different perspective. In circle everyone shares equally, including the teacher, as the talking piece passes from person to person. For many in the group, circle is the first time that teacher and student have been on the same level, allowing for a genuine connection without intimidation or demands for respect. Anxiety diminishes, and each student becomes more comfortable and willing to share. Circle explores unfamiliar territory such as respect, motivation, self-reflection, and accountability. Each topic follows the general theme of positivity. One of the most powerful parts of circle is the final segment, which features each person communicating positive words of encouragement to the person on his left or right. At first, receiving and giving praise was a foreign concept to my students. Nevertheless, by the end of their assigned placements in the Learning Center, these positive words had become their battle cry and their favorite part of circle.

In November 2016, I experienced my most powerful and most difficult circle yet. That day, at the start of my third-period class, which was filled with many Learning Center "veterans," the idea of facilitating a circle seemed nearly impossible. However, I knew these kids were the ones who needed it most. The theme of this particular circle was "the power of words." I began with a basic question: "Do you believe the quote 'Sticks and stones may break my bones, but words will never hurt me'?" As the circle progressed, most students answered that they believed the quote to be true. The talking piece was then handed to one of my seniors. All eyes were on him as he paused, took a deep breath, and said, "I know for a fact that words can hurt and I have the scars to prove it." The young man rolled up his sleeves and showed the scars on his arm where he had cut himself from the torment of words uttered by others. As he began to weep, several students rushed to his aid and told him he was not alone, for they had similar scars themselves. As many began breaking down, the young man went on to explain that he was also grieving the loss of his mother and feared no one would come to his graduation. At this, all the students screamed out, "We will be there for you! We will watch you graduate!" Everyone gathered around to console the young man, with some of them sharing their own stories of losing a parent and how they dealt with it. On that ordinary Wednesday, I experienced an extraordinary moment. I watched a student exhibit an amazing act of courage by sharing his story and saw the response of his classmates rallying behind him. There was not a dry eye in the room.

Restorative Practices shine the light of hope into dark places and give students the realization that they're not alone in their struggles. Some even feel love for the first time. What defines me as a teacher? Hope. Each day, my goal is to give hope, because without it there is nothing my kids can actually learn from me.

Bringing Relationships and Community Back into the Spotlight

If you are reading this book and are a teacher, you likely have experienced the massive shifts in school focus since we were students. Education today is fixated on results. It's easy to understand why. Naturally, we want our students to leave school prepared to be citizens of our rapidly changing country, economy, and world. Unfortunately, students and teachers are judged on the results of standardized assessments. We've jam-packed our teaching schedules with the traditional three R's, but we've lost sight of the most important R of all: relationships. The emergence of Restorative Justice (now called Restorative Practices) in the educational setting symbolizes the need to reclaim and develop the concept of relationships. Fronious et al. (2016, 5) shared the work of Morrison and Vaandering (2012), which describes a system, developed by drawing upon the tenets of Restorative Practices, that values "laws and rules as serving people to protect and encourage relationships and relational cultures," rather than protecting the status quo (145). The status quo, created by this amplified emphasis on high-stakes testing, is what we have struggled with.

Restorative Practices in schools employ a strategy of gathering students literally into circle configurations in their classrooms to discuss a wide variety of issues and thus develop the ability to move beyond that status quo. Four of the main categories of circles, characterized by color cues and names, are Green GTNY (Getting to Know You) Relationship Building Circles, Yellow SEL (Social and Emotional Learning) Circles, Yellow Curricular Circles, and Red Reactive Circles.

Green GTNY Relationship Building Circles proactively create or strengthen relationships. Investment of time and energy toward implementing these goals can lead to a reduction in the conflicts that many teachers struggle with, whether the issues are teacher-student, student-teacher, or student-student problems. I believe that the structure of circle gives us the ideal setting for building, supporting, repairing, and celebrating relationships.

Yellow SEL Circles and Yellow Curricular Circles represent opportunities to engage in positive learning experiences. They offer valuable and effective strategies for social and emotional learning as well as content learning.

Red Reactive Circles are useful in addressing conflicts that have happened or are about to happen. Think about some of the conflicts that you have observed or experienced at your school. The traditional response of the teacher is often to refer the problem to an administrator, who will most likely impose a punitive consequence on the parties involved in the incident and then assume that the issue has been resolved. But restorative conferencing through the circle format can lead to a far more positive outcome. If the teacher is a person who embraces a restorative mind-set, he or she will aim to facilitate a meaningful conversation with all the parties involved in order to repair harm and honor the students' unique needs. Most students need a chance to understand the consequences of their actions and how those actions affect others, and they need teachers who will dedicate time and patience to working with them toward that end.

This book will set forth the ins and outs of all kinds of circles, with a particular focus on the Relationship Building Circle. My hope is that it will become your "go-to" resource for implementing circles in your classroom.

Circles: By Teachers for Teachers

Our ideal audience is teachers who are ready to dip their toes into the Restorative Practices pool and who are interested in the idea of classroom circles. We have learned through our work with countless educators that once teachers discover what circles can offer, they come to value them. I have seen the teacher and administrative training programs that I have helped to facilitate through National Educators for Restorative Practices (NEDRP) be transformed into spiritual experiences as we take participants through

Introduction: How I Found Circle

staff circles that show them how powerful Restorative Practices can be in the classroom.

Teachers leave the training excited about adding circles to their classroom routine. But when they try to facilitate their first circle in their own classes, they may find themselves facing the same dilemma that I did on day one of my initial experiment. They quickly conclude that circles may not work for them. Some may try again and still struggle, just as I did during my first attempts at implementing circles. At this point many teachers may give up on circles because of the initial difficulties, which they may not have realized are common to integrating any new technique into the classroom. We offer this book as a way of being able to walk with teachers through a difficult transition from old habits to new and exciting but daunting strategies. What makes this book about circles special as opposed to other books on the same subject? It's written **by** teachers **for** teachers. We've been in your position, and we understand what it's like to wear the teacher hat.

We've tried to lay the book out as logically as possible. Here's an overview of what the rest of the content looks like:

- Chapter 2, "The 5 Ws of Circle and the Evolution of Classroom Circles," introduces the basics of circles. I will share with you what circle is for me and what it is not. I will outline who participates in circle, where circle can be done, when circle should be done (as in how often), and why we should do circle.
- Chapter 3, "The Facilitator Mind-Set," takes up issues such as demographics, poverty, and trauma. We've learned that the ability to connect with students, leading to authentic rapport with them, has helped us all become more successful educators and circle facilitators.
- Chapter 4, "The Physical Circle," covers the physical aspects of circle, which include the talking piece, the centerpiece, and the circle guidelines. We will share what we have learned about using the talking piece effectively and illustrate its value as a discussion management tool. We'll go over the importance of the circle centerpiece and the power that it holds. Finally, we'll talk about the norms or guidelines that you could develop when deciding with your students how your class circles will run.
- Chapter 5, "The Components of Circle," takes you through Circle Openers, Circle Guidelines, Values Rounds, Discussion Rounds, and Circle Closers. We will share insights into each of these important building blocks for circles and leave you with information that you can easily refer to when creating your own circles.
- Chapter 6, "The Flexibility of Circles: Green, Yellow, Red," elaborates on the many kinds of circles and the many reasons for which they can be

held. We'll describe in detail the four different types introduced above and offer guidance as to which circles you should try first and which ones you should wait on.
- Chapter 7, "Tips and Strategies for Facilitating Circle," is one of the most important parts of the book. This chapter covers circle management. I believe that management presents the biggest obstacle for teachers and in fact is the major cause of teachers' abandoning their efforts to use circles. We offer a number of ideas that have worked for us and many other teachers who have found success in using circles in their classrooms. Here we invite you to learn from the mistakes that we have made. We sure have learned from them!

Between the main chapters of the book you will find a special gift. In the "Circle Mamma's Diary" entries, my great friend and circle mentor Denise Holliday-Jones shares her life, spirit, and wisdom. This gift came about as follows: In the midst of writing this book, I began to feel that something was missing. One night I suddenly awoke from a deep sleep and sat straight up in bed. I could not tell you if I had been dreaming or not, but I recall being wide awake at that moment and saying out loud, "I have to get Denise into this book!" That was the missing piece.

Denise is known as "Circle Mamma" to all of us at NEDRP and to those who are lucky enough to get to circle with her at our trainings. She has worked in public education for more than 20 years as a paraprofessional. She was the Restorative Practices coordinator for Manor ISD at the Disciplinary Alternative Education Program (DAEP) campuses. This involved circling with students, staff, families, and community members. She started as a parent educator at Austin ISD, at the high school she attended, working with teen parents and their families, providing resources and education on parenting.

Part II, "Circle Scripts," offers 20 different models from which you can choose while implementing circles in your classrooms: Nine of the 20 are Green GTKY (Getting to Know You) Relationship Building Circle scripts tailored for various grade levels. Three Yellow SEL (Social and Emotional Learning) Circle scripts provide a glimpse of applying circles to a different kind of learning. Three Yellow Curricular Circle scripts show how to tie relationship building to teaching content areas. Two Red Reactive Circle scripts serve as guidance for addressing classroom conflict. And finally, three Green GTKY Staff Circle scripts detail guidelines for experimenting with circles for staff and faculty interactions.

Part III, "Circle Building Tools," gives you all sorts of ideas that will help you begin creating classroom circles on your own. These have been my go-to materials. I've gathered the question banks and circle activities from many sources, from educators, and from my own experiences.

I am so excited that you're interested in reading *this book*. I hope that the concepts presented here bring you an understanding of what circles can be in the classroom, tips for beginning and sustaining circles, strategies for managing circles, and inspiration to create dynamic circles that your students will love. It's all about relationships. Period. Circles are the most powerful structure that I have encountered for building relationships, strengthening relationships, maintaining classroom relationships, and teaching content. Our students become genuinely excited when they enter the classroom and find that their seats are arranged in a circle. If they see me walking down the hallway with my faithful talking piece, they'll begin asking, "Are we doing circle today?" or "Are you coming in to do a circle with us?" Circles can be the game-changer that you've been looking for.

CIRCLE MAMMA'S DIARY #1

What I Needed from a Teacher

I think back to my time in school, from the primary grades to high school, and I can't help but think that some of my needs were not met. I often think about where I would be in life right now if things had been different for me as a child and teen. Sure, there were academic lessons and concepts that I struggled with. However, I feel that that wasn't truly the area I needed the most help with. What I needed was a teacher to notice me. Not academically, but as a human being. I needed a teacher who took an interest in who I was. Someone absolutely crazy over me.

My home life was difficult when I was a child. Discipline was sometimes unfair and often physical. I think back to third grade. I went to school with a black eye one morning. I can remember the smell in the building. I remember that it was pancake day. My teacher—I can't remember her name, only her face—had to have seen the mark that was left on me. She never acknowledged that the little girl sitting in her classroom was hurt and never said anything to me about it. Maybe it was too difficult for her. Maybe she didn't care. I just remember at that moment needing someone to be there for me. I wanted to yell out for help and comfort, but I knew there would be a price to pay when

I got home. Reflecting back on that day, I now realize what I needed. I needed that teacher to ask questions. I needed her to say, "Hey, are you okay?" or "How can I help you?" or simply "I care about you, I love you." Having a teacher see me as a person would have gone so far for me. It might have driven me to do better academically. It might have given me the courage to seek help. It might have provided comfort from the pain I was encountering at home. Maybe I could have used a kind and reassuring look. A look that told me, "I'm here." These are words that are spoken without a voice but that can be just as powerful as if they were spoken aloud.

As I grew into my middle and high school years, I needed a connection with a caring adult more than anything. Something as simple as a pleasant greeting, eye contact, a welcoming smile. Now I understand that these are parts of developing and keeping positive relationships. I wasn't getting it from home. My mom was a baby that had a baby. Once my dad left, my mom did the best she could at showing me what love is. But she was overwhelmed and often working. I was left to take care of the house. Cook, clean, take care of my siblings. Yet I didn't know what it was like to be in a real relationship or what was needed to build a healthy one. What if I had had a teacher who I felt believed in me? One who cared for me unconditionally regardless of my mistakes and academic struggles?

My concept of relationships with boys could have been much better. In middle and high school, I was getting into boys. I gravitated toward the bad ones. They got attention, so maybe they would help me get attention. This led to many hardships and heartaches that even stretched into my adult life. I could have used a positive relationship with a female teacher. Race wouldn't have mattered. Maybe I needed more love at home. I needed love at school if I wasn't getting it at home. Maybe I would have felt smarter if I had had someone who saw who I really was. I needed a teacher to tell me to love myself, tell me how beautiful I was, and tell me how worthy I was of the very best in all my friends and boys.

At the end of the day, I did not need sympathy from anyone. I needed empathy from my teachers. I needed to have a voice. I needed to be heard. I've been blessed over the past five years to learn and experience so much, thanks to the realm of Restorative Practices. I remember the first circle I sat in; from that moment so much came out of me. Things I had been holding in for decades. I realized in that moment that I had really needed circle as a child. An opportunity to have my voice heard, an opportunity to hear from others, an opportunity to feel like I was not alone. I could have learned that what was happening in my life was not my fault. I could have learned about my classmates. My teachers could have learned more about who I was, my culture, my concept of life. I could have learned about them more genuinely. Relationships could have been built, learning could have been more comfortable, and maybe, just maybe, I could have remembered the name of my third-grade teacher.

CHAPTER 2

The 5 Ws of Circle and the Evolution of Classroom Circles

> Unless you try to do something beyond what you have already mastered, you will never grow.
>
> —*Ralph Waldo Emerson*

I always wanted to be a writer. I enjoyed writing about sports and music while in high school and was a member of the school newspaper club. I started my college career at a two-year college and initially signed up as a communications major with the intention of becoming a journalism major when I transferred to a four-year college. Well, by my sophomore year, this little thing called the Internet burst onto the scene. I saw the writing on the wall (actually, my father pointed it out to me) and realized that the newspaper and print industry would eventually be turned upside down. I did take a handful of communications courses, but I eventually changed paths to education. My journalism classes taught me to use the 5 Ws when creating a news story. Good writers strive to communicate who, what, when, where, why (and sometimes how, although that adds a sixth element and kills the alliteration!) when reporting a story or explaining a new idea to their readers. I decided to use this format (in a slightly different order) to help communicate the circle dynamic.

What Is a Classroom Circle?

The indigenous peoples of North America knew about circles thousands of years ago and used them to spread healing by sharing and by showing respect and honor to others (Living Justice Press). Circles were also helpful for speaking about "differences in heritage, relationships, challenges, stresses, and strengths" among the participants (Bohanon 2005, 92). The circle process of ensuring that each participant has the opportunity to share freely results in a much different forum for communication than does the European tradition, which typically roots communication in spirited debate and favors those who are the most vocal, insistent, and forceful (Umbreit 2003, 1).

In the classroom, circles provide a structure that can foster human connection, relationship building, community equity, and deep understanding of the issues and concerns that are relevant to the group through such strategies as

- meaningful conversation
- curricular learning
- proactive solutions to conflict
- thoughtful reflection
- honest and open sharing
- opportunities to experience, model, and teach prosocial behaviors
- the removal of the "student" and "teacher" dichotomy

The term "classroom circles" elicits a variety of characterizations. Some think that the classroom circle should always be free-flowing and that the content should be organic, created by student discussion and interest. At some times and in some situations this type of circle is ideal. However, we have found that students' participation in circle is stimulated when they are presented with high-quality questions for their consideration. I firmly believe that there is no right or wrong way to plan the parts of circle. Some may prefer to have the majority of their circles, especially relationship building circles, be organic and free-flowing. Rest assured that you will find your own comfort level as a facilitator and develop your own unique interpretation of what circle is, what it looks like, and which components are the most important.

We think it is also important to talk about what circle is **NOT**. Kevin Curtis and Rufus Lott created an excellent document that explores exactly this question (Curtis and Lott 2017). They offer guidance for both teachers and students, through many excellent tips and opinions.

What Circle Is Not . . . for Teachers

- Circle is not a substitute for classroom management. If anything, circle will either confirm or expose whether a teacher can suitably manage classes.
- Circle is not therapy. Although at times it can be therapeutic, it is not designed to delve into a student's deep, dark secrets.
- Circle is not counseling. It becomes counseling only when the teacher wears the hat of counselor rather than that of facilitator.
- Circle is not a time to evaluate a student's response to a question or to coach a student through a question.

- Circle is not an effort to make students cry.
- Circle is not a quick fix. Success cannot be measured by time spent. Circle is a process and may require more or less time depending upon each situation.
- Circle is not a solution for being unprepared. Teachers must treat circle like a lesson and have a plan for facilitating it.
- Circle should not be used only as a reaction to conflict.
- Circle does not have a predictable outcome. Each circle is unique and takes its own shape.
- Circle is not an expenditure of time. It is an investment of time.

What Circle Is Not . . . for Students
- Circle is not a time to be on stage or to be silly.
- Circle is not mandatory. A student can opt out if he or she does not want to participate.
- Circle may not be a time to share things that are confidential or serious in nature.
- Circle is not all about solving problems.
- Circle is not a time to judge other students' responses.
- Circle is not an excuse to miss classes.
- Circle is not always led by the teacher.
- Circle is not a scary process. Students get to choose what questions or topics they would like to answer depending on their own level of comfort in trusting the process.
- Circle is not always for students (or entire classes) that are in trouble.
- Circle is not an assignment, and teachers should not judge or grade responses or participation.

Who Participates in Circle?

All members of the community are invited to participate in circle. Circle should be inclusive and welcoming. Participants may range from preschool children to the adults who spend time in our learning communities. We ask adults to *take their teacher hats off* and to participate as if they are wearing one of their other "hats" in life: as mothers, fathers, brothers, sisters, aunts, uncles, sons, daughters, video gamers, sports fans, artists, musicians, etc. Students may already know us well as teachers, but they yearn to learn more about us and what we are interested in. We'll talk more about the facilitator mind-set in Chapter 3, and that will give you some ideas on how to approach circle.

Circle should never be forced upon anyone. Think about a time in your life when you felt uncomfortable sharing with others or a time when you did not want to talk to anyone. Our students experience such feelings as well. When I invite students into circle, I always explain that the process is voluntary. I'll set up a few places for them to sit outside of the circle if they choose not to participate. I'll often give these students an alternative assignment to work on. I know some teachers and leaders will be skeptical about this idea. However, offering circle as an option (rather than a requirement) gives students a choice and ultimately, and democratically, a voice. In my time as a facilitator I've had only a handful of students request not to participate in circle. I acknowledged and respected these students' requests and let them sit quietly outside of the circle. One of them spent the entire time sitting outside of the circle but still listened as everyone else shared. Another student asked to join the circle once we got to the Discussion Round (I'll explain what this is in Chapter 5). We welcomed her to our community, made sure she understood how circle works, and then continued from where we'd left off. This is something that you may have to experience to believe.

You may occasionally have a student who wishes not to participate for a specific question. This is *absolutely* a common occurrence. Don't get frustrated if a student wants to pass whenever it is his turn to communicate. We've learned that some students need time to build the understanding, trust, and comfort level that they need to feel safe enough to share. I've seen some teachers become concerned when one or more students pass the talking piece. As teachers, we are programmed to expect participation when we ask questions during our lessons. I've found that the quality and age appropriateness of the questions I've asked have been an indicator of the degree of passing. You will get to know your students well, and you will be able to craft questions that they will understand and respond to. Creating circle questions for kindergarten students is quite different from creating questions for middle or high school students!

Why Should We Circle?

The power of relationships is one of the main themes of this book. I believe that circle has been the most effective structure for building relationships that I've used in my career. Relationships create a more peaceful and more connected community in a number of ways.

Circle gives participants unique opportunities to develop the skills that they will need if they are to be successful in this rapidly changing world. Circle gives participants a chance to hear different points of view. The values of different cultures and beliefs can be communicated and celebrated fairly in circle. Circle gives participants multiple pathways for connecting with one another through what is shared. Students get the opportunity to speak in public. Think about how important that is, considering the shift in social communication being heavily weighted toward digital communication. Circle allows participants to speak the way our ancestors did: face-to-face.

We all know that our school leaders are looking for improvements in the educational "bottom line": achievement, understanding, and mastery. We need students to *want* to learn in order to have a chance at any of those three. Relationships created and strengthened in circle can lead to an increase in student motivation and engagement (Roorda 2012, 21). Similarly, the theories of self-system and self-determination investigate student-teacher relationships and student adjustment to school. These theories agree that students become motivated when three needs are realized: *relatedness, competence, and autonomy*. Teachers can promote relatedness by showing genuine interest and being caring leaders. They can boost competence by providing clear guidelines, directions, and structures. And they can foster autonomy by giving students choices and chances to share what is important to them. Circle fits beautifully into these three areas by giving all who are involved the opportunity to learn about one another within a structure that promotes sharing, respect, and honesty.

When and Where Should We Circle? How Often Should We Circle?

Circles can be held at any time of the day. Some elementary teachers prefer circling first thing in the morning, while others find circle to be the perfect way to wrap up the day. There is really no right or wrong time to do circle. Middle school and high school teachers often plan their circles based on the periods when they have class. Some have experimented with facilitating circles during lunch breaks, advisory periods, and study halls.

If you are invested in the idea of implementing circles in your classroom, we suggest that you be very intentional about making time to circle. Elementary settings could find time to circle up one or more times a week. For middle and high school students, aim for trying circle at least every two or three weeks. Consider circle as an investment. As discussed above, well-connected communities with teachers who value relationships create areas that foster increased learning and motivation. Time dedicated early in the year may pay off exponentially by the end of the year.

We've learned that the teachers who tend to struggle the most, or even abandon circle, are the ones who don't find the reason for investing the time.

It takes time for a community (teachers and students) to fully adapt to the circle structure. Intentional and consistent scheduling provides a chance to work through these difficulties. Teachers who schedule a circle only every few months are more likely to eventually discard the process, whereas teachers at schools that invest in circling throughout the grade levels experience an expedited process in which all participants learn and become comfortable with the structure of circle.

As for location, circle can be held just about anywhere. The classroom is the most popular place within a school setting. I've conducted circle in classrooms, auditoriums, gymnasiums, cafeterias, libraries, and even outdoors. Sometimes I have found settings outside of the classroom to be the best places for hosting circle, especially with classes that are struggling with overall behavior issues or classes that have problems with mutual respect. I feel that the classroom may be a stressful place for some of the participants and the change of scenery adds an extra element of comfort.

How Much Time Should I Plan for Circle?

There is really no perfect answer for this question. We are all aware of the attention spans (or lack thereof) of the students we work with. I've facilitated circles in many settings with students ranging from kindergarten to 12th grade. Here is what I've learned:

- For grades K–2, aim for 10–20 minutes of time for a classroom circle
- For grades 3–5, aim for 15–30 minutes
- For grades 6–8, aim for 35–40 minutes (or the length of an academic period)
- For grades 9–12, bell schedules may restrict circle to about 40 minutes. However, I've found that students are quite capable of sitting in circle for 60 minutes or more. Circle ideas can also be extended over two sessions.

By no means are these strict requirements. They simply represent time spans that have worked well for me.

What Does Circle Look Like in a Given Classroom?

We will cover this topic as the focus of Chapter 4. Circles should have seats arranged in a circle, a centerpiece, a talking piece, and sometimes a printed copy of the guidelines that were created by the community.

What Makes Classroom Circle Unique?

Classroom Circle vs. Traditional Classroom Discussion

Circle differs greatly from typical classroom discussion. Classroom discussion usually occurs while students are seated in groups or rows. Most classroom discussion does not have consistent, built-in rituals like circle does. Participation tends to be dictated by the teacher and whoever he or she calls on. The problem with most classroom discussion is equity. Dominant student voices often lead others to choose not to participate. Circle truly gives every student the opportunity to share equally through the use of the talking piece.

Classroom Circle vs. Socratic Seminar

We've modeled circles to hundreds of teachers. I've heard, "Oh, these are basically Socratic seminars!" numerous times. Circle is quite different from a Socratic seminar. First, a Socratic seminar is usually fueled by a text or learning concept dictated by the course that is being taught. The goal of the Socratic seminar format that we have participated in was to help students understand the information being taught. They try to build knowledge of the concept by making statements and answering or asking questions. The dialogue teaches. Most Socratic seminar circles employ an inner and outer circle structure. The students sitting in the inner circle are the students who engage in conversation, while those in the outer circle observe the process and give feedback. The teacher leads and participates but should keep the group focused on the concept and text that are being emphasized. I believe that the Socratic seminar is an excellent structure for teaching content, but please understand that it is not the same as the classroom circle. All types of circles have a shared goal: relationships. Even the curricular circle weaves relationship building into content. Different kinds of circles have very different rituals. Circle gives everyone the opportunity to share and participate for each question and idea.

Classroom Circle vs. Morning Meeting

We are big proponents of morning meeting. Many of the teachers in my school district were trained in conducting morning meeting. The four components of morning meeting (greeting, sharing, group activity, and morning message) do have a built-in relational aspect. Students sometimes will even sit in circle for part of the time. The morning meetings I have participated in last around 30 minutes. I've encountered some teachers who employ a talking piece for the sharing part of the session. Some think that if they do morning meeting they are in essence doing circle. We don't believe this is true. The rituals of each structure are unique to that structure. Circle is all about sharing and getting to know one another. The use of the talking piece is non-negotiable. We are sharing for the entire session.

Don't feel as though you have to choose one format or the other exclusively. I've worked with a number of teachers who valued morning meeting, and we found ways to incorporate both morning meeting and classroom circle into their routine. I've suggested dedicating one or two full morning meetings per week to relationship building classroom circles, especially for elementary-level classes. I've also shown how teachers can schedule classroom circle outside of morning meeting by planning to conduct the two at different times of the day.

CIRCLE MAMMA'S DIARY #2

Courage and Bravery

People often ask about these "circles" that I facilitate and participate in. What are circles? What do they do? How do they work? It's kind of hard for me to give a set answer as to what circle is because it can be different for each individual. To me, circle can be and is a gift. Circle gives those involved an opportunity to let go of things that they are holding on to. Circle can be a time to apologize. Circle can be a time to celebrate. Circle can build deeper relationships with a community. It can be done to introduce someone new to the community. It can heal a community. It can move a community forward.

Circle can be intimidating the first time you or a student sits in one. I vividly recall the first circle that I ever sat in. I was at a Restorative Practices training, with Eric Butler facilitating the circle. Eric was asking us questions that had us remembering things about our past. Emotionally, I was all over the place. When he asked us to reflect on a person who had negatively affected us at some point in our life, I instantly thought of my father. It was an experience that was so powerful that it eventually helped me reconnect with my father after so many years of shutting him out. We had to make it right with each other. I wasn't used to finding a way to make something right with someone, let alone allowing someone to make it right with me. My habits from the past would lead me to building the brick wall, as I had done in this case. This circle helped the process of bringing the wall down. The anger that I had always resorted to now began to make sense. That anger came from pain. My father and I are now closer than we have ever been. Circle gave me the courage to confront these thoughts. Courage I never had before. That courage also gave me a sense of bravery. Courage and bravery work hand in hand. When one gets the courage to address problems, to share openly, to share his or her life, interests, beliefs, it gives one the sense and power of bravery.

As I participated in more circles, I was blown away by what I was experiencing. You mean to tell me that there are people who want to hear from me? There are people who value my answers to questions? I was used to no one valuing what I had to say. This eventually led me not to value myself. In circle I would want to grab on to the insecurities that I would hide behind. Was I speaking correctly? Did I sound as professional as everyone else? Instead, I learned through trusting the process that I could just be me. Just be Denise. I could speak my truth, my testimony, and not worry about being judged by others. I was almost uncomfortable with this dynamic at first. I remember sitting in one of the first circles I participated in and answering a question as the talking piece came to me. As I answered, I waited for someone to cut me off, someone to interject, or someone to correct the language I was using and tell me to say it like this. As my racing mind calmed, I realized that everyone was still and quiet. They were listening to me and what I said. I realized that circle was just as much about listening as it was about sharing. I got to listen to others and realized that I'm not alone in my successes and struggles. I often would think, "Wow, I relate to that" as people would share in circle. Courage led to more bravery. More chances to take that brick wall down. I eventually felt like I needed to take off the victim hat that I had worn for so many years. I discovered that I was not alone in the shame that I carried. I could be brave enough to leave that hat behind me. I knew self-transformation was taking place. I was truly working on me.

Facilitating circle can be frightening when you first try to do it. I had no clue what I was doing when I facilitated a circle for the first time. My son was struggling with his relationship with his father, and I felt helpless. I gave circle a shot. Using a talking piece allowed for my son to be heard and for his father to be heard. And not in the heat of the moment. Looking back at this pivotal event, I really believe the process of circle gave my son and his father the opportunity to understand each other and repair the harm that was tearing apart their relationship. I spoke to my son not too long ago about what he remembered from that circle. He remembered that for the first time he could be heard without being interrupted. See, we can talk. We can talk all day long. But nothing is learned until someone listens. The power of that circle gave me excitement, and it eventually led me to circling with my students at the Disciplinary Alternative Education Program (DAEP) campus.

Every time I circle with students, something special happens. I will tell you, not all circles are as deep and as emotional as the adult circles I participated in and facilitated, yet they are still as powerful for the kids as they were for me. There are so many babies out there who are struggling—some struggling like I was when I was their age, some struggling even more. We need to make time to hear their voices. Let them share about themselves. They will share once they build trust for the process. It may take a few circles, it may not. The things students share will surprise you, will touch your heart, sometimes make you smile, and give you a better understanding of who they are, what their culture is like, and what normal is for them. And let's face it, any voice that comes from a child, with peers and adults sitting around them, can be unexpected. Yet they speak. Many of the kids I worked with at DAEP, and work with now while I am involved with campuses experimenting with circle, live in poverty. Many of our students deal with racism, both intentional and unintentional. They can feel like I did. They can feel like they don't have a voice. They feel like they should just "shut up" and deal with whatever we hand them. These students may not be a disruption in school and may seem to be fine. Giving them the opportunity to be courageous and brave can help build that voice, build that mind that wants to learn and create connections. Circle can be the perfect place to do this if the students choose to trust us enough to participate.

Give circle a chance. Like I said, you will probably feel uncomfortable at first. Remember, it's so important for many of our kids to be heard. Start with getting to know your questions. Build that safe community and prepare for some amazing things to start happening.

CHAPTER 3

The Facilitator Mind-Set

> The time that you spend with your students could be the moment they need you the most, and it may very well be the moment they will remember forever.
>
> —*Crystal Higgs,* Connecting with Students: Strategies for Building Rapport with Urban Learners

A mind-set is a collection of beliefs and attitudes held by a person. The adoption of Restorative Practices requires a mind-set shift for some, since it is based on a relational approach to building culture and climate in the classroom while at the same time responding to individual conflicts as appropriate. This chapter will delve into the mind-set of the circle facilitator.

Authentic Relationships Build Dynamic Communities

Our students look up to us and often learn from us by watching how we act. Students who feel a connection with us will tend to follow our lead. We can't simply assume that they are going to connect with us just because we are their teachers. Connection is earned through the currency of respect. I believe that students are more likely to respect other students, show interest in one another, celebrate differences, embrace and discuss diversity, and show a desire to learn if their teachers authentically model these traits and values themselves. According to Alfie Kohn (1996, 111), "Children are more likely to be respectful when important adults in their life respect *them*. They are more likely to care about others if they know *they* are cared about."

Effective facilitators are skilled listeners, always guiding their students toward success. They observe and relate individual and group strengths, push individuals by offering confident support, and follow through when intervention is needed. They genuinely want to know their students as more than just the people who are on the receiving end of the content that they need to teach. They value the power of authentic relationships and are culturally responsive. Facilitators seek to understand before being understood (Covey 2004).

Circle leaders have the opportunity to educate themselves about the strengths, hobbies, goals, and even fears of the circle participants, and the participants get to learn about the other participants and the facilitator. It's important that our classroom communities understand that we all wear many hats in life. We are not just teachers and students. We learn about one another when we hear about our victories, defeats, and the things that interest us outside of the classroom.

My best experiences with facilitating circles, ranging from kindergarten circles to high school circles to teacher and administrator circles, have occurred when I have shared honestly and deeply. We want the participants to do exactly that, correct? The best way to show them that honest sharing is safe is for us to model it for them ourselves. *Take off that teacher hat!* I know it is difficult for many, and it may make you feel vulnerable. I understand that. Honestly, I worried about that myself when I first started doing circles with students. However, our students yearn for quality relationships, genuine involvement. The best educators realize that a great deal of the learning and progress that take place with our students can be linked to the authenticity of their relationships with us, their teachers. Students want to learn from people they trust. They want to follow people that they respect. They will work hard to succeed for you if they truly believe that you understand them and have their best interests at heart. Students who feel supported by us will be more likely to seek social or academic guidance from us.

My Discipline Plan Starts with Relationships

Boynton and Boynton (2005) believe that strategies to develop positive relationships between students and teachers should be the central component of a teacher's discipline plan. One of the slides we use in training says something along the lines of "I don't have a discipline plan; I have a care plan." If you have a care plan, you won't need to worry much about a discipline plan. To develop a care plan, you have to build rapport with your students. Finn (1989) asserts that school success depends on students' sense of a close connection with their schools. If that connection is present, students believe school is important. Without authentic relationships, they can feel "overwhelmed, criticized, and assessed when they first walk into the classroom. If students do not trust their teacher, then they will experience inhibitions that affect learning" (Higgs 2013, 22). There needs to be trust. Trust should never be expected; it has to be earned. When students see us, their teachers and facilitators, devoting time to building connectedness and relationships in the classroom, they realize that we authentically care about them and that they can trust us.

Connectedness needs to occur on all levels. Hamre and Pianta (2006) emphasize the importance of student-teacher relationships for our most at-risk students, some of whom have very little parental support. This is evident at all grade levels. Transition points, like moving from elementary school to middle school and from middle school to high school, may call for additional investment in building student-teacher relationships. Hamre and Pianta found that middle school teachers who showed "emotional warmth and acceptance" and made sure to communicate regularly and personally with at-risk students saw better connections develop over time. In high school, connection with teachers was more important than connection with family as a factor in predicting specific outcomes. Overall, a student's perceived connectedness with the teacher was the most significant indicator of growth and achievement between eighth and twelfth grades. Circles are an excellent structure for building and reinforcing these relationships as well as for promoting communication among all students.

Culturally Responsive Facilitators

A 2016 report by the United States Department of Education found that 18% of public school teachers in America were individuals of color, and almost half of the students (49%) in elementary or secondary schools were individuals of color (U.S. Department of Education 2016). Such disproportionality can lead to challenges in building understanding, trust, and empathy—three ingredients that are crucial in developing respect.

"Individuals who share the same culture find it easy to connect with one another because there are a great number of commonalities in their behaviors, practices, speech, and much more" (Higgs 2013, 11). Teachers and facilitators who authentically begin to learn about cultures other than their own show individuals from other cultures that they truly want to understand the culture and ultimately want to strengthen their connection with the people of that culture. People form connections when they share details about their lives and about how they see the world. Circle is a dynamic structure for developing opportunities to connect with and learn about one another.

"Students need focused instructional strategies . . . that are designed specifically for their cultural and academic backgrounds" (Delpit 2012, 36). A significant feature of this approach is to emphasize the power of relationships with students. We teachers need to educate ourselves about who our students are, rather than succumbing to society's preoccupation with standardized test performance and thereby focusing on who they are not (Delpit 2012, 37–38). One way to make such a transition in viewpoint is to build authentic relationships with students by embracing, teaching, and celebrating aspects of their cultures, interests, and legacies (Delpit 2012, 49). Tatum (2003) suggests that we create opportunities for students of color to come together with adults to address issues that affect their performance. Circle offers an ideal vehicle for discussing any type of performance (academic, social, physical) and gives us the opportunity to teach about an infinite variety of concepts that include culture.

A. Wade Boykin and Pedro Noguera examine the effects of culture in their book, *Creating the Opportunity to Learn: Moving from Research to Practice to Close the Achievement Gap* (2011). It's a compelling read cover to cover. One chapter of particular interest concerns the importance of interpersonal relationships and asserts that the creation of positive rapport and mutual respect between students and the adults they encounter while at school is one key to closing the achievement gap.

Boykin and Noguera cite a study conducted by Mooney and Thornton (1999) finding that black students, to a much higher degree than white students, "attribute success to rapport with their teachers" (76), an idea that can be traced back in most African societies to traditional thinking about educating the child. In another study cited by Boykin and Noguera, Casteel (1997) queried more than 1,600 black and white middle school students representing the full range of the socioeconomic scale. The participants were asked, "Whom do you most want to please with your class work?" Almost three-quarters of the black students (72%) answered that they wanted to please "their teacher." This percentage was more than twice the percentage of white students who gave the same answer.

Lopez (2009, 5) found that 47% of Latino adults aged 26 or older believe that the difference in cultural background between Latino students and their teachers is a major reason that Latino students are not performing well in school. A survey of Latino youths between 16 and 25 years old revealed that 44% believed cultural difference was to blame for students' lower performance. Students should feel more engaged when they have teachers who are sensitive to the cultural differences that operate in diverse settings.

Boykin and Noguera also share numerous studies that relay the idea that genuine student and teacher relationships develop more often with white students than with black or Latino students. We must find ways to improve and broaden our relationships with these students. The use of circle and Restorative Practices is a step toward achieving this goal.

Understanding Trauma and Poverty

According to the National Education Association, in 2016, 51% of students attending public schools lived in poverty and had a 50% to 80% chance of suffering some form of trauma. Students who endure traumatic experiences may act out as a way of dealing with the associated emotions. Often they come from homes where negativity and discouragement are more prevalent than positivity and encouragement.

The classroom provides a central place for the child and the community that can offer "safety, hope, and healing to families and their children" (NEA 2016, 12–13). To create more healthy environments, we have to be *intentional* and *proactive*. Students whose history includes such experiences can benefit from something as simple as being greeted with a smiling face. We as educators can build relationships with our students that go much further than what we know of them and their situations. These children may feel as though their voices have never been heard by those who are closest to them, those who are supposed to provide for them. The teacher—or, in the case of circle, the facilitator—can become that missing person by creating opportunities for the children to be heard.

Such students struggle with displaying appropriate social and emotional behaviors. Circle, through the input of the facilitator and other circle participants, can model more positive behaviors for the students who will benefit most from learning them. Research has shown that students who have been neglected or hurt can learn modeling through mirror neurons, which fire when a person observes the behavior of others. "Mirror neurons are the way a parent or caregiver passes on humanity to the next generation." Children learn from what they see, and those who have been neglected or abused have not had "normal" experiences consistently modeled to them. Since these children will "copy" the behaviors that they have observed, they may have trouble forming attachments to those who take care of them, and they will likely have difficulty with connecting to adults in their educational settings as well as when they become adults themselves (NEA 2016, 18).

The NEA (2016) offers a number of strategies for working with students living in poverty and those who have been affected by trauma:
- build positive relationships
- create a safe environment for learning
- give students choice
- use a calm voice in the classroom
- teach emotional skills and intelligence
- build short-term memory

- teach expressive writing
- encourage (or "model" or "teach") self-regulation

As you read this book, you will discover that circle covers all of the suggestions listed here. I strongly recommend that you look into current research on trauma and poverty. I believe that it will reveal many keys that can lead to progress on these most important issues.

Testimonial on Participation in an Adult Circle by Adam Benden, LMSW

Adam is a social services coordinator with the Literacy Coalition of Central Texas. He had the opportunity to attend a training for which Denise was the circle facilitator.

My experience with circle was a completely unforgettable and, in some ways, completely revelatory event. During my clinical social work program, I was part of a social justice organizing and action committee mandated by our dean to focus on challenges with diversity and inclusion at our college. There were major issues in our classrooms and a general school climate that resulted in the legacies of racism, sexism, and classism short-circuiting meaningful discussions about social justice among students, staff, and professors. The circle was identified as a possible approach for building community in the school, addressing social justice concerns, and enabling the committee itself to model what we were trying to create by participating in a circle ourselves.

The stories shared and connections made with one another in that circle were startling and unexpected. The trust that a group of mostly strangers developed so quickly was undeniably made possible because of the role and spirit of our facilitator, Denise. Her guidance and modeling of how to speak and listen with openness to others in the group proved to be the foundation for what unfolded over the time we spent together. The spirit and structure of the circle that she exemplified were precisely what made those connections possible, allowing all of us a place to speak about our past hurts and failings and to listen in a way that many of us had never experienced. Perhaps it was inevitable for all of our most personal and intimate stories to bubble up to the surface once we simply had a genuine space to share them. For myself, I know that wounds and weight that I had been carrying for almost 20 years came out in that circle. At a crucial moment, Denise moved from the roles of facilitator and teacher to that of being an equal participant in the circle by sharing a personal story about her son. It was entirely unanticipated, but her story and mine were intricately related. The exchange showed how finding connections through wounds and hurt can provide the opportunity for healing and hearing each other in utterly new ways. Her courage and honesty in that circle inspired my own sharing of my past wrongs and hurt. Our moment of connection in the circle showed me new possibilities for human interaction, trust, and honesty that I never would have predicted. I can honestly say that there was real healing, forgiveness, and the forging of a bond with others in the circle through sharing and listening to one another's stories, and that experience will stay with me for as long as I live.

CIRCLE MAMMA'S DIARY #3

They Say Circle Doesn't Work for Those Kids

Today was amazing. I was working at a DAEP campus. Sometimes we hear people say, "You can't do this on the DAEP campus! The kids don't get it. They're too bad. They don't want it." Coming from a DAEP campus, though, I know that such a statement is furthest from the truth. The teacher that I sat in with today facilitated a circle based on the idea of the power of words.

"Sticks and stones may break my bones but words will never hurt me." That is the way she opened the circle. She asked the students in the circle to think about that familiar saying. She asked them to think about this: "Is this true?" After some thinking time, she began with the first question. "Did the words you used today help or harm someone?" She passed the talking piece, and I heard "help-help-help-help-help" as it made its way around the circle. After the talking piece had made a full rotation, a student raised his hand and asked if he could have the talking piece back. He said, "You know what, I'm going to keep it 100." (This is middle schoolers talking; they mean they'll keep it 100% real.) "My words probably hurt somebody today. I probably didn't use good or kind words. I called people names. I'm sure my words probably harmed somebody." After that, the talking piece worked back around the circle. This time, I heard some variance. The majority of the students started to say that their words harmed others.

The next question was a surface question about how we try to push past the words that hurt us and how we try to be impactful with our words. One student got the talking piece and talked about how the word "ugly" was often used in class.

She moved on to this: "Now, I would like us to use our words to say something kind to someone. Something to affirm them. If you're not comfortable, you can write it on a sticky note and give it to the person later." The teacher then talked about herself. "I think my words probably harmed someone today. I got really upset. You guys got me mad and I began to yell. I just want to affirm that you guys forgave me and still love me through that." This was the teacher! How powerful for students to hear this, and such a great way to model the power of accountability. The next kid got the talking piece and looked to another girl in circle. "I've known you since we were like three or four years old." The student who was being spoken to, Brianna, looked a little uncomfortable and defeated at first. "I want to affirm you because you are always so positive here and you try to make friends with everybody." I could see the student giving the compliment try to leave the comment at that. She paused. "But I want to apologize because I've been mean to you and I've said ugly things to you. You are friends with everyone and I felt that you should have only been friends with me. I hurt you and I made you sad. I want to apologize to you for that." Brianna's eyes filled with tears.

Another boy asked for the talking piece after that. "I want to affirm myself because I'm so handsome!" We all had a great laugh at this. The next boy got the talking piece and right away he said he was nervous. You could see his cheeks turning red. I heard him whisper, "Oh my God, I have trouble with this stuff. My heart is racing." He didn't know what to say. The next person in the line for circle was an adult, and he said, "I can share what I have to say!" I said, "No, we wait on people in this process. It's when they're ready. It's not about us." I returned the talking piece to the student. "I want to say thank you to one of the girls in class." He looked at her—I can't remember her name—and she smiled and turned red.

At the end of the circle, I found myself drawn to Brianna. I walked over to her and noticed that she still had tears in her eyes. I asked her if I could hug her and she said yes. She grabbed me as if it was the last hug that she would ever give. I said to her, "Tell me about these tears."

I didn't want to ask her if she was sad or happy. I didn't want to make an assumption. She said, "It just really felt good to get an apology because most people don't apologize to me." I felt something behind me as she was saying this. It was the girl that had apologized to her. She then went and hugged her. Brianna burst into tears. What a powerful moment. The trust that was formed in circle gave the students the opportunity to seek forgiveness and the opportunity to experience redemption.

The power of this work, and of circle, is indescribable. There are times when I meet teachers who don't find the value of circle. If the kids are "tough," they may be less likely to attempt the process. We can't get into this attitude like we can't work with these kids or they don't want it. Our thoughts can become our actions. I've found that the "tough" kids are the kids that need this process the most. They are the ones who do justice to what Restorative Practices and building relationships are all about. Imagine how comfortable these students feel around their teacher. She chose to create the space for these conversations, and by doing so she created the canvas for an authentic community based on understanding, honesty, trust, and forgiveness.

CHAPTER 4

The Physical Circle

The key to a successful learning environment is structure.
—*Cara Carroll*, The First Grade Parade

Equality is evident in the shape of any perfect circle. All of the points in a plane that are the same distance from a point called the center point create the curve of the circle. The measurement from the center point to any of the points on the outer edge of the circle is called the radius. The radius is equidistant from the center to each of the points on the circle's edge regardless of at which place a point appears on the circle. In Chapter 4 we will explore the center point of the classroom circle, which is called the centerpiece. We will also discuss the talking piece, which is an important physical object that identifies the speaker.

When preparing for circle, try your best to actually arrange the seats in a circle. Sometimes my circles look more like ovals than circles, but that still works. Most of the literature recommends keeping the circle free of barriers. This may be difficult for some who have large desks in their learning environment. To address this issue in my classroom, I would have the students flip their desks 180 degrees, then sit on the desktop and let their feet settle on the desk seat. Some teachers may not be comfortable with this setup. I've seen some teachers arrange bulky desks in a large rectangle going around the room. This is not an ideal situation, but it can still work. I have occasionally hosted circle in a horseshoe shape when using a screen for showing visuals. I would usually place my seat blocking the screen. This allowed me to keep the circle for discussion and then pull my seat aside so participants could look at the screen when the time came. Ultimately, you, as facilitator, must decide how to set up circle.

The Game-Changer: The Talking Piece

The use of a physical object, known as the talking piece, is one of the key parts of classroom circles. The talking piece acts as a symbol that identifies the speaker at any given time. It is passed either clockwise or counterclockwise once a question or idea is presented to the group. A participant with the talking piece is allowed to speak and share with the community. Participants without the talking piece have the opportunity to listen and learn from the person speaking. The talking piece keeps the class focused on the question or idea that has been presented. The hope is that students will feel safe enough to participate and share genuinely. It's through this safety, along with opportunities to listen to different viewpoints and opinions, that we hope the community builds strength, responsibility, and respect for one another.

Think about a normal lesson or discussion in your classroom. Usually a handful of students participate consistently, and some even dominate the discussion. The talking piece creates a more equitable environment for learning, sharing, and participating. When introducing the talking piece to teachers we call it the great equalizer. Participants in our circle trainings are often skeptical about student involvement in the circle. They fear that the students who are often quiet, shy, or withdrawn will be less likely to want to share when the spotlight and the eyes of the community are focused squarely on them. For the most part, however, we have experienced the exact opposite. We have observed that those students who are the least likely to speak up in regular class discussion may become the most vocal participants, with deep contributions for the circle discussion. I wish I had kept track of how many times I have had teachers come to me after I have facilitated and share their total amazement about how a specific student spoke up in circle and said something impactful.

Something also happens with students who may be accustomed to dominating classroom discussions or being the ones who fool around too much or consistently disrupt the class. Teachers participating in our NEDRP experiences often worry that those students will either dominate the circle discussion or purposely try to sabotage circle. I've found, however, that overall, the exact opposite happens. Think about students who are intent on dominating the classroom conversation. In a regular class they can do so because it's easy; all they have to do to accomplish their goal is raise a hand or shout out unexpectedly. The talking piece takes these options away. What about the student who you are worried won't take the talking piece seriously? We've found that something interesting happens when a talking piece is employed. The spotlight shines brightly on the student who is waiting for

The Physical Circle

the talking piece to make its way to him or her. These students usually crave an audience in class, but when they get the audience, especially when all eyes turn to them by virtue of the physical setup of the circle, they tend to get stage fright. It's easier to goof around in class when the seating arrangement is set up in rows or in small groups of desks. The circle configuration has a way of holding everyone accountable to the same guidelines and agreements and allowing everyone to see what is going on. I've genuinely found that these formerly disruptive students actually can become shy and quiet. It's one of the most interesting social dynamics that I've encountered in the classroom.

Let's talk about what can serve as a talking piece. One tip right away: Don't use a full-size basketball when doing circle with a group that can be very active. I learned that the hard way! The facilitator is often the one who chooses the talking piece. I have my faithful bamboo stick that I use for my talking piece much of the time. It was created by a teacher who was artistic and inspired by the idea of doing circle after he went through our training. It had symbols that looked like hieroglyphics that were added by paint pen. My sixth-grade students were drawn to the art on the talking piece and always had questions about it. The stick is about 15 inches long and has been a perfect talking piece for facilitating circle with middle school and high school students. However, it's not the most ideal talking piece for younger elementary students. It's hard, it makes a loud noise if it's dropped on a tile floor, and it can hurt a young student if it is not handled with care while passing it. For younger students I like to use a small stuffed bear. My younger daughter, Emma Jo, purchased the bear at the Conklin Flea Market and gave it to me for Father's Day a few years ago. I share this story with each new group of younger students. They enjoy it and get the chance to hear me talk about how important my kids are to me.

Be creative when choosing your talking piece. It does not have to be the same object for every circle. You can choose a new talking piece for each circle if you like. I recommend that you try to choose an item that has special significance to you, the group, or the topic that is going to be discussed. It can add value, intrigue, and greater understanding for the circle you are going to facilitate. You may offer a number of talking pieces and have someone from the circle select one and explain why he or she chose it. You could have students bring in their own talking pieces.

The Power of the Circle Centerpiece

When I first started facilitating circles, I did not see the importance of creating a centerpiece for the circle. I would simply put the chairs or desks in a circle and start the session. It was not until I began working closely with NEDRP that I discovered how valuable centerpieces are for any type of circle. A centerpiece is created by placing a mat, cloth, flag, poster board, or some similar foundation on the floor in the middle of the circle. The facilitator carefully chooses a number of objects and arranges them on top of the mat. The objects may help tell a story about the facilitator, the participants, or the topic to be discussed.

The first time I used a centerpiece, I immediately experienced the value of it. Students walking into the classroom instantly gravitated toward the display and started talking about the objects I had placed there, asking questions like "What is this?" "Is that your daughter?" "Is that your wife?" "Is that your favorite team?" The arrangement grabbed their attention and got them interested in what we were about to do. An intriguing aspect of the centerpiece is that it's not a static, unchanging feature of the circle landscape. Once the students understand what it is, they themselves often enjoy adding objects that are important to them. You can place items within the centerpiece for just one circle and then switch some or all of them out for others as desired. The ideas, possibilities, and look of the centerpiece are endless. Be creative and think of what will pique the interest of the circle participants.

As an example of constructing a centerpiece, I'll describe one that I set up for a relationship building circle with a new class. I have found that when I'm preparing to circle with a new group, building a centerpiece that tells my story is beneficial and quickly creates bonds between me and a group that I do not know. My centerpiece background for this situation is a New York Giants flag that I did not have a flagpole for at my house. On top of the flag this time I included the items listed below. I've explained why I chose it and what I hope it tells about me.

- A framed print of my engagement photo: *I want the community to see that I am married and that my marriage is important to me.*
- A framed photo of my two daughters: *I want the community to see that I am a father and that my children mean so much to me.*
- A New York Mets World Series cap: *I want the community to learn that I am an avid New York Mets fan and that I have been since I was in the third grade (bless my heart).*
- A framed photo of my brother and me at the World Series: *I want the community to see that I am a brother, an older brother, and that we are best friends as adults.*
- A Syracuse basketball jersey from 1987: *I share that I love basketball and*

The Physical Circle

> that my grandmother, who passed away in 1990, got me interested in the sport and this team. I want the community to see that I love sports and that my family is and has been important to me throughout my life.

- A pair of soccer shin guards and goalie gloves: *I share that this is the sport that I've played the most in my life. I share that I still play and that I continue to practice to get better. I want the community to see that I still have passions and that I still work hard to improve my skills in these hobbies.*
- Two video games: Halo *and* FIFA soccer, *in the middle of the circle, grab student interest immediately. It's a great way to show how I (as an adult) have things in common with our learners. I want the community to see that I have hobbies outside of school, just like they do.*
- A photo of the first class I ever taught: *I began teaching in 2001 and still have the class photo of that group. They are all adults now! I want the community to see that they will be important to me even when they have moved on.*

As you may have noticed, I was intentional in choosing what to include in my circle centerpiece. I want the circle participants to be able to look at the centerpiece and see a group of objects that tell a story about me. I really want them to see that I have interests, inside and outside of school, and that I'm a person even when I'm not being their teacher or circle facilitator.

You would be surprised at how well the students remember the parts of this centerpiece. At one point I piloted relationship building circles with fourth- and fifth-grade classes at one of our elementary schools in Binghamton, New York, for about seven months. I tried to meet with each class (there were three) at least once a month. I used my faithful centerpiece for the first set of circles and then decided to try to freshen it a bit for the second visit. I added a few new pieces to the centerpiece and took a few old ones out, then waited for the students to return from their music class. They entered and were excited to see that I was there and that we were going to be doing relationship building circles. We started with a circle opener, then went over the circle guidelines and revisited the use of the talking piece and centerpiece. I told the students that I had replaced three of the objects in the centerpiece and asked them if they could identify the new pieces. The first three students who volunteered named them easily. I then asked them, "Can you remember the three pieces that I took out?" Again, the first three students who volunteered got it right. One month later, they again remembered what had been in my centerpiece and what had been taken out. Pretty impressive! And it was not only one class that did this. The other two classes that I worked with were just as successful in identifying the new pieces and recalling the ones that had been replaced. I felt that my goal of wanting the students to learn a bit about me had been achieved just by strategically choosing objects that they could relate to for the centerpiece.

Centerpieces may look different in different types of circles. For example, I participated in a combination relationship building circle and curricular circle, facilitated by Scott Schwartz, that included both relationship building material and concepts that were taught in the classroom. Scott, a humanities teacher at East Middle School in Binghamton, was instantly intrigued by doing circles in his classroom. He facilitated a number of relationship building circles during the first month of the school year, and as the class got used to the norms and guidelines of circle, he decided to experiment with teaching curricular concepts by using the circle structure. He created a curricular circle that covered the First Amendment of the Constitution and related it to methods of communication that his seventh-grade students used in their own lives. Students entered the classroom and were attracted to the centerpiece that Scott had created. He had laminated a number of images that were relevant to the topic. There were large photos of the icons that represented some of the social media sites that students used, including Facebook, Snapchat, Twitter, and Instagram. He also had a photograph of the students who were the focal point of the Supreme Court case *Tinker v. Des Moines Independent Community School District*, which was heard in 1968. A picture of the president and statements that are associated with the First Amendment were part of the centerpiece. Students were abuzz before the circle began as they talked about social media sites. Scott's selection of relevant pieces that could be part of the centerpiece created student excitement and spurred them to begin accessing their prior knowledge of how they communicated with one another. Utilizing prior knowledge led to wonderful circles in which students were able to learn about one another's beliefs in a respectful manner.

CIRCLE MAMMA'S DIARY #4

Creating a Positive Environment

The talking piece and the centerpiece are such valuable parts of circle, not just for the role they play but for the messages that those two things can send to the participants. The symbol of the talking piece and the contents of a centerpiece can set a tone for circle. They both can tell a story, share a thought or feeling, and have significant

The Physical Circle

meaning to one or more people in the circle. I've seen a number of circles facilitated without a centerpiece, and I felt that they were missing out on a great opportunity for the students to deepen the connection with one another. I've also seen special talking pieces that brought to the surface stories and teachings that made circle much more powerful for all. I have my "go to" centerpiece when I circle with adults or students for the first time. My centerpiece includes photos of my family. The images may change from time to time, but I always have pictures of my children. I also include pieces that other facilitators have given me. These objects, which can be used as talking pieces, often have been given to me as tokens of endearment and connectedness.

I've been thinking about the many circles that I have facilitated and/or have been a part of over the years and the centerpieces that I have either put together myself or have seen others share. I want to share with you the centerpiece I used at the state conference in October 2017. I was meeting with a group of more than 40 people and wanted to take them through a circle. I decided to do a fishbowl circle, which meant we took about a dozen people and put them inside the circle. The rest of the attendees sat on the outside of the circle so they could observe the process. I decided to include a picture of my stepson in the centerpiece. My stepson was the student in school who was often in trouble. He was frequently suspended. He had learning difficulties and struggled academically. Home was not ideal for him. His father was the only working parent. His mom was taking care of him mostly, but she had her own struggles. The school would call home when issues came up, but his mother was so lost in her own difficulties that the importance of the phone calls did not resonate. The system, and even life itself, was failing my stepson. He ended up spending too much time out on the street, which got him connected with the wrong people. Back home, Dad was working and Mom had her own stuff. The elements of the street were quick to find my stepson. He's in prison now, and it breaks my heart.

So, back to the centerpiece. I had some other items in the centerpiece that shared a little about who I am (more about that in a bit), but in the middle of the circle was the picture of my stepson. I intentionally had his picture facing down when circle started. Before I picked it up, I told his story. I explained that his picture was turned over because we lost him when we had the chance to make a difference in his life. By "we," I mean the system, notably the education system. I finally picked up his picture and held it so everyone could see him. I looked into everyone's eyes as I showed it. We used that picture as the talking piece. As we shared, I watched the participants look at this picture with understanding and love. The message of finding a way to relate to all of our children came out in so much that was shared. The circle became an emotional experience for me, those who were participating, and those who were watching from outside the fishbowl. My sharing this story helped connect us on a spiritual level. It opened me up to them. And in return, the participants opened up to me. Establishing an inviting atmosphere helped send a message that circle was a place of trust and acceptance.

A great centerpiece and talking piece can help circle participants open their lives to one another. Sometimes we need to put it all on the line, even with our students. That may sound horrific to some of you, and it was for me too at first. I found that once I took my teacher hat off and opened up to my kids, the connection was powerful and authentic. Sharing our hardships and celebrations with our students lets them know that we trust them and that they are important to us. At first the students may not make eye contact with you when you share deeply, but in the end they look at you, invested in what you are sharing, instead of looking over you. This is a path to true connection.

In my experience, students, before adults, "jump in" to circle when we create the environment for all voices to be heard. When kids learn about our lives, interests, and struggles, they can connect to the point where they have our back. Once, in a student circle, a participant asked if anyone had ever lost anyone close to them to cancer. A student shared that a loved one had fought cancer and talked about the pain it had brought. The talking piece then moved to another student. This student said he had lost his dad to prison due to the cancer of drug abuse. Another shared how his uncle was in prison. So many students in this group had lost someone to disease or incarceration. There's power in sharing the stories. If the students are struggling, they realize, "Oh, my God, I'm not alone." Those who aren't struggling get the opportunity to experience empathy. At the end of circle, so many students continued talking to each other and offering support. I heard,

"It's okay, I'm here for you," and "If you get sad you can come talk to me." What a powerful way to connect with each other.

I experienced the use of another especially meaningful centerpiece while participating in a circle that was facilitated by a teacher on a campus that NEDRP supports. The teacher's centerpiece included a collage of pictures with her son. She then shared with me that her son had recently been killed in a car accident. Her students were aware of this, as they had used this collage in the centerpiece before. The students really honored and respected their teacher. As they focused on the centerpiece while they talked, they saw what their teacher really loved but also what she had really lost. They could be present in circle because of what was placed in the center.

When we are intentional in sharing about ourselves, and letting the circle participants share about themselves, we create a positive environment for circle. Most students will share when they feel safe and connected. A powerful centerpiece and talking piece can help us share our lives (or if the students choose the centerpiece/talking piece, it helps them share their stories) and create pathways for connection, understanding, respect, and trust.

CHAPTER 5

The Components of Circle

Every child deserves a champion, an adult who will never give up on them, who understands the power of connection and insists that they become the best they can possibly be.

—Rita Pierson, educator, TED talk speaker

Circles are fantastic structures that can be implemented in any classroom, faculty meeting, professional development session, business meeting, and countless other forums where people meet to collaborate. The circle concept seems simple when you read about it. I remember hearing an administrator in a district mention that his staff ran circles. I asked him how they went about introducing circle, creating content for circle, developing an environment built on respect, and closing circle. He simply said—and I'm paraphrasing, since this conversation took place a few years ago—"I just tell my teachers to circle up with their students. Put them in a circle and talk with them." Now, can you run circle like that? Sure, I suppose you can. Sometimes circle can be just an organic gathering where the students decide the topic. That kind of circle runs well when the students respect one another, when they understand what a talking piece is and how to use it, and when they agree upon a number of guidelines and values. I was skeptical, however, that there was any type of validity in implementing circle within this administrator's building. More than a year later, I checked in with him and asked how circles were going with his staff. He admitted that the staff had given up on doing circles because they either did not see the value in spending time on them or thought that from a classroom management or behavior standpoint using circles resulted in more work. I was not surprised by this outcome.

I've learned through my own experiences in facilitating hundreds of elementary, secondary, and adult circles that participants crave a flexible but

The Components of Circle

consistent framework within which to do circle. Regular use of a talking piece and a centerpiece not only strengthens the content that circle can cover but also creates familiarity through the physical objects that are part of circle.

There is no one correct way to organize the activities and questions of a circle. I've seen a number of books and presentations that set up circles in different ways, for different purposes. A reactive circle created to focus on solving a problem that is occurring between two groups in a community, for example, will be quite different from a relationship building circle aiming to establish trust among students in a sixth-grade classroom. And even then, if I facilitate relationship building circles in five different sections of sixth-grade classes during the same day, no two will be exactly the same.

In this chapter, I am going to share with you what has worked best for me in helping teachers create dynamic circle guides, or scripts, to aid them in conducting circle. I suggest that facilitators develop a circle plan that follows the components of circle. The plan doesn't need to be set in stone, though. It serves as a reference tool for teachers, especially useful if they hit an unexpected snag and don't know exactly how to respond. Sometimes circle will send teachers down a different path from the one in their initial plan, especially when a circle participant spontaneously shares an interesting topic, idea, or emotion. In such situations it's fine to depart from the plan to take advantage of the moment.

The main components of any circle are as follows: Circle Opener, Circle Guidelines, Values Round, Discussion Round (with questions that may range from shallow-ended to middle-level to deep-ended), and Circle Closer. I'll go in depth with each component and share successful examples. Part II of this book, "Circle Scripts," contains 20 sample circles of all sorts. Each component is also featured in Part III, "Circle Building Tools," which includes a list of tested activities for Circle Openers and Closers, banks of questions that can spark discussion in the Values Round, and an extensive collection of topics appropriate for the Discussion Round. This wealth of material will prove an invaluable resource as you begin creating your own circles.

Circle Opener: Setting the Scene

One of my favorite parts of the Olympic Games, whether summer or winter, is the opening ceremony. It usually presents a theatrical show that highlights the culture of the host nation. Then the athletes, grouped by country, march into the stadium. The grand finale of the ceremony is the lighting of the Olympic torch, after which the games commence. This impressive spectacle gets me excited and prepares me for the whirlwind marathon of sporting events that will consume my time for the next two weeks. Enchanted with the splendor of it all, I sometimes find myself watching competitions that are completely new to me (curling? trampoline?).

The opening ceremony of the Olympics can easily serve as an attractive analogy for the opening of circle, signifying and celebrating the beginning of something special. In getting themselves to circle, students are often transitioning from a learning environment that does not follow the guidelines of circle. The circle opener provides an opportunity to get them in the mood for circle. We start each and every circle with an opener.

This initial activity does not have to be time-consuming. It can be as simple as a quote. Sometimes it can be an image. Poems are an excellent way to open circle as well. I try to find something that is relevant to what we will be talking about in circle that day, preferably something that will strengthen the central theme or topic. It is often important to break down quotes and poems for the students, help them understand the message. You could ask them what the quote, picture, or poem means to them. I've found that students are intrigued with the backgrounds of the authors or artists who created the item that we're exploring, so I try to educate myself before circle so I can answer questions that may come up. Making a few slides in PowerPoint, Google Slides, or Keynote that can be displayed on a screen (if you have access to a projector) is always a great idea. A slide can show an enlarged image of a quote or poem. It can show a photo of the author or a good view of a painting. For example, I've used a number of Shel Silverstein poems as circle openers with elementary students. I type the shorter poems out and project them on the screen as I read them to the students. They are always intrigued by Silverstein, as I still am, so I add a slide about him with a photo of some of his books that we have in our school library. (I would bet that you would see a few of his books come in after a school library visit by the students who heard about him in circle!)

Using games or activities as circle openers is another option. One of my favorites is the Weather Report. This activity employs the talking piece. Ask circle participants to describe how they are feeling by relating a weather type to their mood. If a student is having a great day, he may say that he's feeling sunny. A student who's in a bad mood may say she is feeling stormy. I once had a student explain to me that he was a rainbow. He said that the day had started out badly but since had improved greatly. Pretty creative! You can also incorporate the Weather Report into the centerpiece. Here's how: Create a poster with a few weather categories like sunny, partly sunny, cloudy, and stormy. Place a sticky note on the chair of each student in circle. To start, have the circle participants, one by one, place the sticky note in the category on the poster that describes how they feel. This activity gives you, the circle facilitator, an idea of each person's mood. The whole opener takes just a minute or two. A similar activity, called Fist-to-Five, can also be used to gauge the mood of the circle participants. Have students hold up fingers to show how they feel. One finger is something along the lines of terrible. All five fingers is fantastic. You could extend the Fist-to-Five by using the talking piece and having students explain why they chose the number of fingers that they did. This is another opener that should take no more than a minute or two (if you pass the talking piece). A quick tip about the facilitator's role in this kind of activity: Be real! If you're having a lousy day, let the students know. Show one finger in Fist-to-Five or say you're feeling like a hurricane. (One participant in a Dallas, Texas, training told me, "I'm a roaring tornado!")

One of the most useful overall tips I can give you is to take your teacher hat off and put on your real-person hat. The students will relate to you better. Let them see that you are human and that life isn't all sunshine and flowers. I'll even tell them why I'm stormy. Maybe it was an argument with my wife, maybe I overslept, or maybe my favorite team lost last night. Regardless, be as real as you can. Students will often follow what the facilitator models. If you're willing to be real, they'll be more likely to be real.

As mentioned above, Part III offers many opening activities and games to get you started. I've gathered these activities throughout my many years in the classroom and over the past three years while facilitating and modeling circles for countless teachers. Some of the activities I've created myself. Others were shared with me by teachers who used them in the classroom. Please reach out to me (johnjwhalen@texrp.com) if you have a great circle opener that you would be willing to share. I would surely appreciate it!

Circle Guidelines: Developing the Procedures of Circle

One of the most important parts of facilitating powerful circles is the creation of circle guidelines. Without guidelines, participants will not know what the expectations are. Some call this component "Circle Rules" or "Circle Norms." I prefer "Circle Guidelines" because they are the description of "best practices" for participating in circle. The guidelines you set are specific to the group, or groups, that you meet with. Guidelines are best adopted by the group rather than dictated by the teacher or facilitator of circle. I myself found success by introducing four guidelines for approval in my circles, as follows:

1. Respect the talking piece. If you have the talking piece, it is your opportunity to share. If you do not have the talking piece, it is your opportunity to listen and learn about the other members of our

THE INS AND OUTS OF CIRCLES

community. You may choose to pass the talking piece if you do not want to share.
2. What is said in circle stays in circle. We want to build a community where we feel safe enough to share. Sometimes we will share things that are personal. We need to be able to trust one another. So what we say here stays here.
3. Safety: If you share something that makes me think that your safety is in danger I must report it by law.
4. Speak from the heart! I hope that you will feel comfortable enough to share openly and honestly with the group. Say just enough to share your part and be considerate of others and their opportunity to share.
5. Is there a guideline that you feel that we need to add to our list? (This is not a guideline, but it is something that I ask the class. You may want to ask students to raise their hands for this one, or you can pass the talking piece around.)

I go over these guidelines explicitly EVERY time we meet in circle. It does not matter if it is the first time or the 50th time. Reviewing the guidelines reminds everyone of what is needed for a successful circle. Sometimes I'll ask volunteers to share the guidelines. Other times I may begin a guideline and have the circle participants finish it in chorus. I say, "And another guideline of circle is, 'What is said in circle . . .'" and they finish with "stays in circle!"

Over time, I learned a valuable tip for reviewing the circle guidelines. Following each guideline, I ask the community of participants for affirmation of the guideline. I ask students to give me a thumbs-up if they understand the guideline and if they are willing to try their best to follow it. I scan the circle and make sure that EVERY student gives me either a thumbs-up or a thumbs-down. Using the "thumbs" method turned out to be a great time-saver, and it also creates an opportunity for holding one another accountable. Let's say that there is a student, or a group of students, who are struggling with respecting the talking piece. Instead of lecturing the class, or singling out particular students, a circle facilitator can stop the circle for a moment and use an affective statement (an I-statement) to remind the class of the guideline:

"Folks, I have to pause the circle for a moment. At the beginning of circle we went over the guidelines of circle. The first guideline had to do with respecting the talking piece. If you have the talking piece, it is your opportunity to speak. If you do not have the talking piece, it is your opportunity to listen. I'm confused about this because when I asked the members of the circle if they were good with this guideline and would put their effort into trying to follow it, I got a full circle giving me a thumbs-up. I just want to remind you that we need this in order for circle to run well and to run in a way that we are all respected and valued. I truly feel that no one came here today to try and make circle run poorly. I just wanted to remind you that we really need this to happen. Can I get a thumbs-up if everyone understands the guideline and will try their best to follow it?"

Believe it or not, the use of affective statements, like this one, has been overwhelmingly successful in helping me manage minor disruptions in circle. I've found it much more effective to make a statement to the group as a whole than to single out the student or students who are creating the disruption.

Speaking of thumbs-up, my good friend Kevin Curtis shared with me a tip that has been invaluable in building consistency with the use of the talking piece. Students often break the talking piece agreement not out of intentional disobedience but because of their excitement about what is shared. They perk up when they hear another student share something that is relevant to them or is something that they have in common with the student who is speaking. A student may yell out, "Yeah, me too!" or "Oh, I like that!" or even "I have one of those too!" Such exclamations show that they are engaged and excited. They're listening! They just need a way to show their excitement without violating the talking piece. Kevin suggests using the "thumbs-up" signal to help with this. Students are encouraged to give a thumbs-up to the speaker if they like or are excited about what is said. What if they REALLY like what is said? Well, give it two thumbs-up! (We discourage the idea of using thumbs-down as a response to questions, since that can attack the goal of respect and trust.) I revisit this tip, along with other strategies for managing circle, in Chapter 7.

One final detail regarding the circle guidelines: In New York State we are mandated reporters. The New York State Office of Children and Family Services (2016) defines the role of a mandated reporter in the "Summary Guide for Mandated Reporters in New York State" as follows:

> Mandated reporters are required to report suspected child abuse or maltreatment when they are presented with a reasonable cause to suspect child abuse or maltreatment in a situation where a child, parent, or other person legally responsible for the child is before the mandated reporter when the mandated reporter is acting in his or her official or professional capacity. "Other person legally responsible" refers to a guardian, caretaker, or other person 18 years of age or older who is responsible for the care of the child.

I do not read this verbatim to all of the students who participate in my circles. However, I do go over it EVERY time I review the circle guidelines with circle participants who are minors, regardless of age. I explain to them that if I or any of the other adults who are participating in circle feel that their safety is compromised or that they are in danger, we must report it. I tell them there is a law stating that I must report issues of safety. I want them to know that I would feel terrible if I failed to help them in a situation where their safety was at risk and I knew about it. I want the participants of the circle to trust me. We speak about "what's said in circle stays in circle" and how the possibility that I may have to report what they tell me contradicts this guideline. I often give younger students an example, or sometimes multiple examples, of something that would cause me to report, by using this story:

"You walk to school every day. There is an adult who has been bothering or harassing you as you walk by him each day. He threatens to hurt you, another child you are walking with, or someone in your family. I need to find a way to help you and keep you safe. I would speak to the appropriate professionals to get you help and to keep you safe."

I also explain that they could be in danger because of the way they are treated at home. I let them know that I could face formal charges if I fail to report anything that falls under our state's requirements for mandated reporting. Each state should have a specific protocol for mandated reporting for professionals working with students. I strongly advise that you consult your state literature or speak to a central administrator in your district who is up to date on the specifics of such legislation. In the end, you want to make sure that the students understand this. I'll often tell groups of students to think about what they want to share in circle. If they feel that what they are sharing may reveal that they are in danger, I will ask them to speak in private to me or to another adult that they are comfortable with, and we will take the necessary steps to help them.

It may seem tedious that we review the circle guidelines at the beginning of each circle. I get that question at almost every training when I'm facilitating teacher circles. Some worry that doing so will be too time-consuming. Others worry that any enthusiasm that the students may have brought into circle at the beginning of the session will be lost by going over redundant guidelines. However, it's a useful practice because it brings to mind guidelines that may not have been discussed in some time, it reinforces the equality of the community by stating how we treat one another, and it shows how much you, the facilitator, care about the safety and well-being of the circle participants. Reviewing guidelines is also an excellent proactive technique for managing circles because you can address possible "bumps" before they even happen. This strategy may take a few minutes when you first begin to use it, but eventually it will become a routine part of circle and will take much less time.

Some teachers have found it beneficial to post the circle guidelines in large print at a highly visible location in the classroom. Such positioning makes it easy to refer to the list during verbal reviews of the guidelines. Be sure to leave space on the sign to add further guidelines that circle participants may propose over time. Don't just laminate it and leave it. Live it!

Values Round: Identifying What Is Important

Identifying and understanding the values that are held by a group of circle participants is a crucial step in building an environment that fosters genuine sharing, trust, and mutual respect. Values rounds are particularly important when introducing circle to a new group, so be sure to plan enough time to figure out values during the initial meetings. You will notice that each of the sample circle scripts in Part II of this book features unique questions for the values round. After the group has completed the foundational work of identifying its values, the values round in circle can serve as a chance to review those stated values, thus reinforcing and extending the group's comfort level with the idea of meeting in circle.

Any number of questions could be asked to help participants determine what their values are. The "Values Round Questions" list in Part III offers many ideas. There are also a number of creative ways to handle the values round in circle. As an example, I'd like to share one of the best values round questions that I've used when facilitating circle. It's a question that Denise Holliday-Jones shared with me, and it illustrates why Denise has earned the nickname Circle Mamma: she takes circle to a whole other level. On this occasion she and I were sitting in a circle made up of adults (teachers and administrators) who were learning about circling, and she asked this question: "What do you need from this community so that you can share openly, honestly, and with your heart while in circle?" She gave the group about 30 seconds of thinking time. (A huge tip: Give the group a bit of thinking time before passing the talking piece!) Each participant used a marker to write what he or she needed on a white paper plate, then signed the plate on the back and placed it on the floor nearby. Once everyone had completed the task, the talking piece was passed around and each participant shared what he or she had written, then pushed the plate toward the centerpiece of the circle.

I was amazed at what this group of adults, many of whom did not know one another, shared. Some of the needs that I heard stated were the following:
- Please don't laugh at what I share.
- Share honestly.
- Keep confidentiality.
- Respect my needs even if they are different from yours.
- Try to share. It makes me more comfortable sharing if others share also.

I began to use this values round question each time I met with a new group, and it was a game changer. As the facilitator, I would jot down what people were sharing. Once everyone had shared, there would be a number of paper plates around the centerpiece. I would get the talking piece back and read out all the values and needs that the participants had identified as important. Then I would ask the group if they were willing to respect all of these values. I asked that each participant who was willing give me a thumbs-up. The values plates were clearly displayed around the centerpiece and could be quickly accessed if the values needed to be revisited. A facilitator could even make a sign for the classroom or circle environment with these values stated on it. A values round activity for a future circle could be to quickly review these values and needs before moving to the next topic.

Discussion Round: Crafting the Questions That Guide Our Conversation

I remember writing my first lesson plan as an undergraduate at the State University of New York at Geneseo in 1998. I can still recall the components that I had to include in order to create a lesson plan that would be to the professor's liking. There was the objective, which stated the desired outcomes and learning targets of the lesson. There was a category for materials and time needed. Then there were the anticipatory questions, with which we began the lesson and that we used as a way to grab the students' interest. After that came the bulk of the lesson, or the "procedure." This outlined the activities step by step, the "teacher talk," and the transition to the lesson closure. The discussion round of a circle reminds me of the procedure section of a lesson plan. The questions that guide the discussion should be phrased to address whatever concept, idea, or objective that the facilitator desires. This is especially important in curricular circles and SEL circles. The main objective of relationship building circles is creating and strengthening relationships within a community, and the questions selected by the facilitator can support the achievement of that objective.

Circles don't always go perfectly. Participants may not want to share, for

The Components of Circle

a variety of reasons. They may feel nervous about being honest and open with their peers; they may be concerned about a lack of sharing by others; they may find the questions to be difficult to understand or relate to. We have found success using a strategy that NEDRP founder Kevin Curtis shared with me. Kevin describes three types of questions that we use: shallow-ended questions, middle-level questions, and deep-ended questions. An understanding of where the circle is in emotional terms at any given time helps us to decide which types of questions to ask. Remember, we create scripts to help us with facilitating circle, but many times we stray from the script according to where circle leads us. Let's take a look at the three types of questions and why each type is important.

Shallow-Ended Questions

Shallow-ended questions are questions that do not have much emotional or intellectual depth. They are easy questions to answer. For younger students—K–2, for example—a shallow-ended question could be something as simple as "What is your favorite color?" Other shallow-ended questions:

- What is your favorite time of day?
- How old are you?
- What is your least favorite food?
- Where would you travel if you could choose any destination?
- How would you spend $100?
- What is your favorite game?

Through their responses to these easy questions, circle participants learn quite a bit about one another. I always remind groups that they can discover pathways to getting to know one another by finding out what they have in common. Maybe two students find out that they have the same favorite game. Boom! Connection made.

Asking questions at this level can also help teachers to understand their students better. Think of a student that you have, or have had in the past, who was difficult to get along with or who sometimes made your life as a teacher challenging. That student may share something when answering a shallow-ended question that allows you to see him or her in a new way. For example, take the question about what you would spend $100 on. I once asked this question, then listened as the talking piece went around. Many of the students answered as would be expected: candy, sneakers, video games, movies, bicycles, and so on. Then the talking piece got to the student who had the most difficulty with meeting classroom expectations and struggled greatly with the challenges of being in positive relationships with his peers. This student took the talking piece and explained how he would give the

$100 to his mother so that she would not have to worry about gathering enough money to buy groceries for his family. That moment was a revelation for me. I saw this student through an entirely different lens for the rest of the year. I felt like I understood him better just by knowing his situation. His answer to that shallow-ended question contributed to the beginning of a strong relationship with him and resulted in fewer problems in the classroom for both of us.

Shallow-ended questions serve another important purpose as well. The ease with which students can answer these questions helps them get ready to share when we move on to questions that are more specific and possibly more serious. In my first circle with a group of kindergarten students, for example, we did a fun circle opener and a simple values round, and then it was time to start the discussion round. I wanted them to see how the talking piece worked, so I started the circle with this question: "Tell me what your name is." That was it. The students were eager to answer and to watch the talking piece travel around the circle. I followed that question with, "When is your birthday?" Students quickly answered that question as well. "What is your favorite food?" They were excited to share this in the circle. Three quick shallow-ended questions got them sharing, gave them experience with the talking piece, and prepared them for more in-depth questions to come.

I almost always aim for one or two shallow-ended questions at the beginning of any discussion round. It's fun to come up with shallow-ended questions when creating a curricular circle or an SEL circle. In Part II, "Circle Scripts," I've included a curricular circle that I did for a ninth-grade English class. The topic that the classroom teacher and I wanted to address was arguments and counter-arguments. The teacher gave me full rein to facilitate and to produce the circle, since it was his first time to see a circle in action. I decided to use a local issue in our community as the circle topic. The Marcellus Shale Formation sits beneath our area. The state border between New York and Pennsylvania lies about 15 minutes from our high school. About 10 years ago, natural gas company representatives started knocking on the doors of Pennsylvania residents near the border and offering them vast amounts of money for permission to lease their land. Many Pennsylvanians made a fortune as a result. For circle, I wanted to start with a shallow-ended question that would get the students ready to answer higher-level questions about fracking and their opinions of it. I began by showing a fictitious $100,000 bill on the projector. I explained that the students were Pennsylvania residents and that a representative from the gas company would be knocking on their door with a check for $100,000. The money would be theirs; they themselves would have to perform no work to receive it. The question: "What would you do with that $100,000?" Well, the answers were fantastic! Students shared a variety of ways they would spend their money. I was surprised that so many of these ninth graders chose to save most or all of the money. This shallow-ended question put them in the shoes of their neighbors, raised their interest about what was next, gave me the opportunity to gauge what might be important to each student based on what he or she shared, and got just about everyone using the talking piece. It was perfect and led to one of the most enjoyable circles that I've ever facilitated.

Middle-Level Questions

Middle-level questions are questions that ask circle participants to reflect on and share their opinions or understandings. They are threaded into the discussion following the shallow-ended questions. In a relationship building circle, these may be questions aimed at getting students to consider a specific topic relevant to the community. For SEL circles and curricular circles, the questions may be intended to get students to relate their prior knowledge of the circle topic to a subject that will give them the opportunity to connect what they already know to new learning.

Deep-Ended Questions

Deep-ended questions are questions that take us to deep emotional places. Participants may feel comfortable enough to share very personal stories. These stories, or comments about them, tend to bring the community closer together. You truly have to experience it to understand it.

I've been surprised when I've seen a question that I considered to be a shallow-ended or middle-level question turn out to be a deep-ended question. We once asked a group of teachers at a training what we thought was a shallow-ended question: "Do you have a pet?" The talking piece made its way around the circle and then landed in the hands of a participant who became choked up. He explained that his dog had recently passed away. He took the time to explain why that pet was important to him and why he had experienced so much difficulty after the death. The circle participants were very supportive of the grieving member. Many shed tears themselves. The willingness of this person to share forged a strong bond over the two sessions that this group spent in circle. We also found that after that experience, others shared very deeply.

One thing that we've learned is that we never want to leave circle in the deep end. We want to see participants leave with smiles on their faces. An important task of the facilitator is to gauge where circle is in this regard and, if it is in the deep end, try to move it back to the shallow end before the conclusion of the session. This can be done by choosing a shallow-ended question or by selecting a circle closer that will bring the group to a happier place.

Circle Closer: Identifying the End of Circle

Recall our discussion of the opening ceremony of the Olympic Games. The conclusion of the games is marked by a closing ceremony. Similarly, we want students to understand when circle is coming to an end. At that point I often praise the participants for their effort and their willingness to share with one another. These moments can provide an opportunity for me to support the students in whatever they may have shared. It's also a good time to talk about when the next circle is scheduled to be and discuss ideas for topics.

We always close circle with intentionality, just as we open it with intentionality. The closing may offer more time for an activity or game, depending on how much time has been used for the other components. Some activities may work just as well for the opener as for the closer, though some ("21" and "Count to 10," for example) work better at the end of circle than at the beginning.

CIRCLE MAMMA'S DIARY #5

The Power of Values

I've had the privilege of either facilitating or participating in hundreds of circles with both adults and students. I particularly enjoy facilitating the adult circles that are part of our NEDRP experiences. A few years ago, John Whalen had the opportunity to be part of an adult circle that I facilitated. Afterward, he came up to me with questions. "Denise, what is it about your circle that made it such an amazing and connecting experience?" We spoke about his circles, and it sounded like they were similar to my circles. I asked him if he used a values round, and he said he didn't because he wasn't sure about what the values round was. I wasn't too surprised by this because I've noticed that the values round is absent from a lot of circles. I explained to him that the values round can set a tone that allows the community to feel that they can genuinely share. I told him about one of my favorite questions for the values round: "What do you need from this group today in order to feel like you can share openly and honestly?" He ran with this question and said it was a game-changer when it came to establishing trust with the community. I really think we do an injustice to the kids (and adults) when we don't include the values round. It's easy to skip. Sometimes it's time-consuming. However, offering the chance to share and listen to values can take circle to a wonderful place.

The Components of Circle

The values round offers each person the chance to say what he or she values while letting the community know what values are important to the overall group. I often ask participants what value they are willing to bring to circle. I hear all types of values. Everything from participation to confidentiality to being nonjudgmental. I've seen something interesting as a result of asking this question: the value that participants are willing to bring is often the value that they need most from the group. If someone is bringing trust, they may also need to receive that same value. In an adult circle that I did, I asked this question about what value each person was bringing to the circle, and a lady got the talking piece and said that she brought trust to the group, while being nonjudgmental was the value that she needed. When I asked the first question of the discussion round (which follows the values round), I could tell that this lady was very uncomfortable with circle. "I really don't do this," she said. "I'm not used to talking like this in front of adults." I could see her beginning to get red in the face. She quickly passed the talking piece to the next person. She wanted that talking piece out of her hand that instant!

This continued for a few questions. Then, slowly, she began to share. It took her a while to put her thoughts together. She later told me that she was not used to people being patient with her when she was sharing. However, in this circle everyone was patient. Everyone listened intently. No one was judgmental. She began to share more comfortably and confidently, and by the second circle we did, which was on the second day of the training, she was really open and shared really deeply. At the end of circle, she came up to me and hugged me tightly. Honestly, I had not been sure whether she would show up for the second day because she was so uncomfortable on the first day. She told me that she had actually thought of not coming back that morning, but that now she was so thankful she had come. We talked about the values that she shared. She said that she brought patience to circle, and she sure did. However, when I thought about it, I realized that she also needed patience from the people in circle and the facilitator when it came to her feeling comfortable enough to open up in a way that she was not normally used to.

The values round can give us an understanding of a particular person's culture. It can tell us about where they come from, what their beliefs are, and what is important to them. It can tell us about the culture that they actually live in, which is their home life. We are all unique! Connection can happen when we listen and learn about all of the values that we have in common and the values that we may differ on. This is where I believe we are struggling in both the classroom and society. We are not respecting the values that we need and the values we bring to our communities. Everyone brings value and everyone should be respected.

I didn't understand what my value was until I came into this work. I knew that I was a value to others, but my true value, what I value as a person, allowed me to see what my purpose in life was. That purpose is connecting with others and celebrating human connection.

I've found that for students, the values round exposes their non-negotiables. This is especially true with our students who struggle the most with relationships and trust. It's like they are saying, "If I'm going to do this—participate, share openly, step out there for you—then this is what needs to happen." Compared with adults, students can be much more open and honest when it comes to sharing. They just need to know that their values will be respected. Setting values, for many of them, is really just trust building. It kind of gives them a chance to size us up. They can find out if we can be trusted, if we can value different points of view, and if we truly want to learn about who they are. They can find out if we trust them enough to share our stories with them.

When we share values in circle, we outline what we need and what we can bring to the group. I've found that our kids do a pretty good job when holding themselves accountable for the values round if the facilitator takes the time to speak about and explore values. I once saw a teacher write the value the students shared on their name tags. This was a powerful act and brought values outside of the circle. Students and adults can learn: if my value is being respected, then respect is being given. I advise teachers to take note of the values that the students share and use them outside of circle as much as possible. Knowing what each student values can help us differentiate instruction and interactions according to the specific needs of the individual.

CHAPTER 6

The Flexibility of Circles: Green, Yellow, Red

> One looks back with appreciation to the brilliant teachers, but with gratitude to those who touched our human feeling. The curriculum is so much necessary raw material, but warmth is the vital element for the growing plant and for the soul of the child.
>
> —*Carl Jung*

Circles can serve as powerful structures for discussing and exploring a wide range of topics. This chapter will focus on four types of circles that fit nicely into the classroom setting: Green GTKY (Getting to Know You) Relationship Building Circles (both students and staff), Yellow Curricular Circles, Yellow SEL (Social and Emotional Learning) Circles, and Red Reactive Circles. The accompanying color designations supply cues that aid in characterizing each type of circle. For example, green circles offer opportunities to develop relationships and interpersonal dynamics within the group. Circles labeled as yellow are more oriented toward content, curriculum, and different kinds of learning. A circle described as red represents a problem area, an issue that the group must address and resolve in order to move forward with the development of the circle.

Green Classroom GTKY Relationship Building Circles
(Circle Scripts 1–9)

The following is just a short list illustrating the flexibility of green proactive circles, which can be effective in
- promoting peace within a community or classroom
- establishing classroom norms
- building or strengthening community
- making decisions

- teaching content
- checking in
- welcoming back someone who is returning after an extended absence
- introducing a new member to the community

Classroom relationship building circles are gatherings within a classroom that value open sharing and discussion. Their focus is to create an equitable forum in which personal relationships can be built or strengthened. This type of circle can help a teacher understand the students in ways that most classroom structures don't allow. Successful relationship building circles are rooted in mutual trust and respect. Deep sharing can occur and often does. Classroom relationship building circles provide a platform for celebrating both our similarities and our differences. They keep us tuned in on what is happening in one another's lives and provide a structure for discussing what is important to the classroom community. These circles usually begin with the teacher as facilitator. Eventually, once the community embraces the values and guidelines of circle, students themselves can (and will want to) serve as facilitators. Relationship building circles work well for classrooms, school advisory groups, sports teams, and even staff meetings.

Using this format to build authentic relationships can create a community rooted in mutual respect and provide valuable tools with which the group can address the conflicts that will inevitably arise throughout the year. These circles are proactive classroom pieces. The dividends of devoting time to building relationships are realized when situations need to be addressed reactively. Recall the introduction to this book and my experience of bringing circle to my sixth-period class. The investment in developing relationships and understanding in that situation created a currency of respect and trust. The mutual respect helped to effectively navigate the bumps encountered along the way. As mentioned earlier, circle itself is not a classroom management tool or a behavioral program—though that is a common misconception among those who are interested in introducing circle to their classroom or community. Rather it is a structure or vehicle for learning. If a teacher struggles with classroom management, he or she will also struggle with facilitating circle.

Finding time for relationship building circles at the elementary level is much easier than in higher-grade-level classes in which students move from classroom to classroom throughout the day. For three wonderful years when I first began teaching, I taught second grade. We would start each day with 30 minutes of carpet time. We'd read poems, review the date and note the important things on the agenda, and play community-building games. This was my version of a morning meeting. I know that many teachers do use the

The Flexibility of Circles

morning meeting in their classrooms, and I have sat in on many as I have visited elementary classrooms throughout my district and across the country.

Having observed those situations, I need to reiterate an earlier cautionary note to teachers: Please don't confuse a morning meeting with a classroom circle. To be sure, there are similarities. For example, morning meetings frequently offer a time for discussion. I've even seen a few teachers use a talking piece, although most I have spoken to do not. In contrast to morning meetings, the classroom relationship building circle follows a certain structure (discussed in Chapter 5): Students sit in a circle. A talking piece is used. Preferably a centerpiece is placed inside the circle. There will be enough time to ask more than one question. The teacher will open and close the circle intentionally, as a regular part of its structure. In reviewing circle structure here, I am by no means suggesting that teachers should not do a morning meeting! As noted earlier, I truly found great value in following a morning meeting protocol. My message is that you can do both!

For middle school and high school students, planning time for relationship building circles is trickier, since they typically change classes according to a bell schedule. My good friend and colleague Keith Bernstein and I wrote a pilot program a few years ago that implemented a number of structures that support a Restorative Practices philosophy at our school. We asked our pilot team to experiment with the inclusion of relationship building circles in their classrooms. We were asking new teachers to dedicate one full day of instruction (five instructional periods over the course of the year) to experiment with relationship building circles. We wanted to take it slow so as not to overwhelm our teachers. Almost all of our pilot teachers conducted at least four relationship building circles throughout the year. We learned that doing a relationship building circle with a class every 10 weeks was less effective than we had hoped. The meetings needed to be scheduled more frequently. I've since suggested that classrooms at the middle school and high school levels hold relationship building circles every two or three weeks to start with.

Eventually, this kind of circle can lead to powerful curricular circles that can cover both content and relationship building simultaneously. We found that investing exclusively in relationship building circles at first helped to build community in the classroom, as well as familiarity and acceptance of the process, after which the transition to the curriculum circle model was basically seamless. One tip for teams of middle or high school teachers: Communicate with your fellow teachers about when you plan to hold circle. My experiences over the past few years have proved to me that students enjoy circle and are excited to participate in it. However, like anything else, too much of a good thing can be result in saturation. Students may grow weary of circle if they do it in three or four different classes on the same day. To help avoid such scheduling issues, we've created weekly planners for circle that teams of teachers can share when setting up circles for multiple classrooms. Be creative!

Some middle schools and high schools have advisory and conferencing periods built into their daily schedule. At the middle school where I work, for example, we have a 20-minute advisory period each day. The idea behind scheduling this period was to provide a home base for our students. We do not have a formal homeroom period, and our students move among eight or more classrooms a day. The advisory groups all have about 10 students and an adult. The adult may be a teacher, a teacher's assistant, a guidance counselor, a social worker, or even a school psychologist. I decided to hold just about every advisory meeting in circle. My group that first year was quite an experience. The 10 students represented the epitome of diversity on a socioeconomic and academic spectrum. We had strong personalities, and as I quickly discovered, there were few, if any, existing relationships among the students. It was a slow start. It took a few weeks of patience, consistency, and even courage before we saw the magic of relationship building circles begin to emerge. Seemingly out of nowhere, our circles really began to take off by mid-October. Students began to listen to one another, ask questions, and show real interest in what others were sharing. It soon became my favorite time of the day. We eventually built a structure for how we wanted to do circle each day and what we wanted to discuss. We would do a quick circle opener, review our guidelines and values, and jump right into the discussion round. This is what our week looked like:

- *Monday*: Check in from the weekend. We'd share what we did, who we saw, even what we ate!
- *Tuesday*: Question Bank Day. First I would display a list of 20 random questions on the screen in front of circle. Then I would randomly draw a name and have the student pick a question that was interesting to him or her. If none of the questions in the list seemed appealing, students could create their own. (See Part III for a substantial question bank that you can mine for discussion questions.)
- *Wednesday*: This was the one day when we might not have circle. Often we were given a lesson in social and emotional learning. I got really good at translating that outside lesson into a circle discussion.
- *Thursday*: We'd talk about our experiences at school. This was a slow-moving effort when we first tried it, but it became a valuable part of circle. I would give students a printout showing where they were academically, behaviorally, or attendance-wise. We'd discuss what bothered us, what we struggled with, and what we thought solutions might be.

The Flexibility of Circles

- *Friday*: This was our celebration day. We'd celebrate our successes and our perseverance from the week that was ending. We'd share what we were excited about for the weekend. Every four or five weeks, I would bring in a treat for the class. Sure, it cost $5 or $10 each time, which may not be an option for everyone, but in my experience, gathering to share a snack served to strengthen our bond even more.

I would often have conversations with my colleagues about their advisory periods. A number of them were struggling with holding students' interest and keeping behavior under control during this time of day. Some were so frustrated that they concluded the period was not getting the results that were intended. This was in total contrast to what I felt. For me, circle provided the perfect forum for creating real relationships. By the end of the year, I knew so much about my group. My students loved being in conferencing. A few days before the end of the year I started circle by saying that I'd like to share what I knew about each of our students. I spent 20 minutes talking about the lives of my 10 advisory students. They enjoyed it, and many laughs were shared.

As I wrapped up that circle, one of the students said, "Hey, don't we get to say what we know about you?" I had never thought of that, so I agreed that the next day they could pass the talking piece and share what they knew about me. The next day came, and we proceeded as planned. Each student shared something different about me. One student went into the makeup of my family and reviewed all of my family members' names and what I liked to do with them. Another told about my love of being in the woods and my hobbies of hiking, mountain biking, and camping. They kept going on and on. I was blown away by how much they remembered about me. If I had never shared deeply with my group they would never have gotten to know what I'm really all about outside of being a mathematics teacher. The love and interest shown to me by my advisory group left me teary-eyed and sad that the year was ending. Fortunately, the relationships have continued, even though we no longer meet every day. We stop and share a quick word or a conversation while passing in the hall. I ask them about their video games, their karate practices, their cheerleading competitions, their Sunday dinners, their families, and so on. I check in on how they are doing with their teachers. I consider our group a family, and I'll give full credit to the structure of circle for leading us there.

I strongly suggest that people experiment with relationship building circles before branching out to the other types of circles that we will address in upcoming sections. As you've seen from earlier accounts in these pages, circle does take practice. Many teachers are eager to do circle but want to add curricular circles, SEL circles, and reactive circles immediately. I've found that most of these teachers struggled when jumping in with both feet right away. As I noted earlier, some found the effort so difficult that they discarded the use of circles altogether. The teachers who have been successful in implementing the higher-level circles have almost always first invested time in establishing a solid foundation in relationship building circles.

Alternative Types of Relationship Building Circles

Relationship building circles do not have to be time-consuming processes, though it may be difficult for middle and high school teachers to carve out the necessary niche for circle. Here are two suggestions for circle structures that address the time issue.

Step-In/Stand-Up Circles

This kind of circle takes very little time, can be done with large groups of students, and requires no talking piece. Here's how to do it: Have the students who are going to participate quickly form a circle in the room. Explain to them that you are going to make a series of statements, one at a time. If they agree with the statement, they take one step into the circle. Those who step into the circle are saying that they all share that idea or concept. I like to start with shallow-ended questions. I'll say, "My favorite food is pizza," and then step into the circle. I may then look at the other people who stepped in and ask them a follow-up question. Maybe something like, "What is your favorite type?" or "Do you prefer square pieces or triangular pieces?" Then everyone steps out, I ask the next question, and the process is repeated, slowly moving into more serious or even deep-ended questions. A community of learners can find out quite a bit about one another in very little time by following this format. I've been able to do five or six statements in less than five minutes.

I've also come up with one valuable strategy for facilitating such quick encounters. I like to make a statement that I myself can step in for. By putting myself in the "yes" or "true" part of the circle, I may make it easier for a student to participate. Consider the question "Do you know anyone who is struggling with substance abuse?" Students may be reluctant to step in for this question but may feel more comfortable if they see me stepping in.

A variant of this type of circle, if you have the time, is to have each participant (or a set number of participants) make a statement. As the facilitator, start with a statement yourself and give those who agree the opportunity to step in. Then pass the responsibility (and you can use a talking piece for this) to the next person. This modification of the procedure allows a number of people the chance to choose the content.

The Flexibility of Circles

Two-Minute Connection

Another effective structure for learning more about your participants and giving them a voice in circle discussion is the two-minute connection. Take a moment at the beginning of the week to have each participant write a question or topic on a slip of paper. Put the slips in a container. Then pull one slip each day at the end of a lesson or before a transition. Have students stand in a circle around the classroom and then announce the question or topic. Use the talking piece and begin. You should be able to make a full circuit of the room in about two minutes.

How about some advice? Make sure you read all of the submissions yourself at the end of the day on Monday. You'll immediately get a glimpse of what is on the minds and in the hearts of your students. Maybe there's a topic that appears numerous times. This can provide ideas for future circles. Previewing the slips also gives you a chance to remove any inappropriate submissions. I worked in middle school for a long time, and I can assure you that such things do happen! Also, don't have participants fill out slips and then never pull them for discussion. Students may not record important topics if the facilitator never pulls the slips. I suggest refreshing the slips at least every two weeks.

Testimonial on Relationship Building Circles by Doug Overton

I have known Doug since we facilitated a training together in 2017. A Teacher of the Year for his district, Doug associates Restorative Practices, specifically relationship building circles, with his success.

In the fall of 2016 my principal asked me to go to a district-wide behavioral training to find ways for our staff to build better relationships with our students. During one of the sessions, a member of National Educators for Restorative Practices (NEDRP) spoke on Restorative Practices, challenging everything I thought I knew about discipline. I had been an advocate for bringing back a stronger sense of discipline to our schools, not realizing that punishment wasn't actually getting results. I left that training with a new mind-set. As I started implementing some of these strategies in my classroom, I began to see my students differently.

One of my favorite circle success stories is about a skateboarder and a football player finding common ground. Eric was an introverted young man with no self-esteem. He came to circle each day with his head down and a heavy heart. He felt that no one cared about him. Ryan, a very extroverted and passionate young man, was the life of the circle. These two people, with entirely different personalities, had an impact on each other that neither will forget. During circle, Ryan always encouraged Eric never to doubt himself or to let anyone bring him down. Even beyond circle, he made it his mission to include Eric in every aspect of class time. Eric began to see himself as worthy of a friend. He came out of his shell and began speaking his own personal words of encouragement to others. On Ryan's last day, Eric shared that the person he respected most in this world was Ryan, because Ryan had believed in him when nobody else did. At this everyone in the entire circle began to tear up, and Ryan and Eric shared a moment that no one would forget. Ryan learned that he was more than an overbearing and misunderstood jock. He became a leader by using his enthusiastic disposition to influence others in a positive way. Eric found his voice, and to this day he encourages all the other students better than anyone I have ever seen.

After the successes of my students, my principal asked me to lead a staff development session using the new strategies I was implementing in my classroom. The feedback from the other teachers was extremely positive. I became the campus Restorative Practices coordinator to assist teachers with implementing these strategies in their own classrooms. As the year progressed, I led multiple staff development sessions on Restorative Practices. This training helped equip our staff with tools from TEXRP, such as relationship agreements and classroom circles. I was also charged with facilitating all reactive circles when conflict arose.

The results for that first year were no less than astonishing! The recidivism rate declined, and in-school suspensions were significantly reduced. In the friendlier environment, students' anxieties diminished. I believe the Restorative Practices project will have a lasting impact on my students and their future successes.

Testimonial on Relationship Building Circles by Scott Schwartz

Scott, a good friend of mine, is a seventh-grade U.S. history teacher at East Middle School in Binghamton, NY. He immediately saw the power in classroom circles and uses them more than any other teacher in our district. He is a very effective facilitator and is becoming a great curricular circle writer.

I have facilitated a lot of circles this year and plan to have many more. The most powerful circle I've done (so far) was one that gave students the opportunity to ask questions of me and about me. At the beginning of the circle we reviewed our values, norms, and circle procedures, including what the talking piece is and what it represents. Then I gave each student a sheet of notebook paper with the instruction to write down two questions that he or she wanted to ask me. If more questions came to mind as the talking piece went around, the students could write those down and ask them as well (time permitting). As the subject of the circle, I was to decide how deep I wanted to take the circle with my answers. In some classes, I stayed relatively shallow. In other classes, I really took it deep and got into some details of my life that I wanted to share in hopes of making connections with students who usually don't have deep connections with their teachers. By the end of the day, I was drained, but I left school with a feeling of "this is going to be a good year."

Testimonial on Relationship Building Circles by Sarah Coutu

Sarah was a teacher in the Richardson ISD in Texas for two years. She now works for NEDRP as a trainer.

My first impactful circle was in the fall of 2017, when I substituted for a coach/ISS teacher. I was in the ISS [In-School Suspension] room ALL day with three young men. These young men were in ISS for various frivolous reasons. I knew that it was going to be a long day, so I took a shot in the dark, whipped out my centerpieces and my talking piece, and asked these boys to join me in circle. I explained to them what circle was, what my job with TEXRP was, and said that I just wanted to help pass the time in a meaningful manner. The boys did not hesitate at all; to them, my idea seemed much better than putting their heads down or copying the class rules all day long.

Now, what's said in circle stays in circle, of course, but lessons that come out of circle conversations can be shared. After THREE HOURS (that's right, three hours) of circle, I felt like those boys were my little brothers. I knew every single one of their stories, struggles, and celebrations. They shared things that I would never have imagined they would have had to go through as teens. I had attempted to conclude circle after 25 minutes, but the boys were so completely immersed that they begged to continue and even came up with their own questions, better than anything I could have thought of.

You know what caused me to become even more invested in this process? It was the fact that the boys wanted to circle AGAIN after lunch. I figured that they just wanted to waste time and make it pass faster, but they actually wanted to share more. All three of them wrote notes to their future selves, which blew me away. One of them even stated that he was planning to stop smoking and asked the rest of us to hold him accountable on that.

When I say that this was one of my best days as an educator, I am not exaggerating. All three boys hugged me tightly before they left, all three asked for my e-mail address so they could keep in touch and invite me to their games or just share their celebrations with me, and all three have e-mailed me since.

If my own account of the story isn't powerful enough, take it from the mouth of one of the students: "Miss, I wish my teachers would do this. None of my teachers know any of the stuff I shared with you. They just don't get it and they yell for no reason. I wish they would do this the first day of school since we don't do anything that day anyways because if you were my teacher and we did this same thing, I would have no problem listening to you teach!"

I know that my role as the ISS teacher was to take their phones and have them sit quietly or do busy work all day, but I think what I did had more impact on the boys than a day of busy work ever would. In the end two of the boys applied for jobs while in my class, and both did a mock interview with me to practice their interview skills; one applied for a college he was thinking about; one (on his own) decided to stop smoking weed, and the other two encouraged him AND gave him tips on how to stay busy and away from his family members who smoked it. Ultimately, those boys had found someone who cared to listen to them for more than just that one ISS day.

Green GTKY Staff Relationship Building Circles (Circle Scripts 18–20)

Relationship building circles are not just for classroom communities. They can also be powerful connecting structures for the staff of a school. Marzano, Waters, and McNulty (2005, 59) identify building effective relationships as one of the 21 responsibilities of a school leader. Fostering and supporting administrators and teacher leaders can result in circles that provide opportunities for staff to create or strengthen relationships that allow them to share the happenings of their lives, to identify the needs of teachers or students, to discuss important school information that typically would have been presented during a traditional faculty meeting, and to celebrate the efforts of all stakeholders in this community. According to Lewin and Regine (2000), as cited by Fullan (2001, 52), "When the individual soul is connected to the organization, people become connected to something deeper—the desire to contribute to a larger purpose, to feel they are part of a greater whole, a web of connection." Staff circles should look just like classroom circles. We use the same physical components and planning structures for both kinds of circles.

In the course of facilitating dozens of staff circles, I have found that they can be powerful experiences. I recall the first staff circle that I facilitated at

The Flexibility of Circles

the middle school where I was teaching. We divided the staff of about 60 into 5 random circle groups. Participants included building administrators, teachers, teacher assistants, guidance counselors, school psychologists, and the school nurse. I created a circle script for four other staff co-facilitators to refer to as a guide. I recall that when the staff members read the script that I gave them, they were nervous about asking some of the questions. They were worried that the staff would turn circle into a complaint session. In hopes of avoiding that outcome, we worked together to build on the questions that I provided before the meeting.

The meeting started with a brief introduction explaining why we were doing staff circles. After that, the groups adjourned to the rooms where the circles had been set up ahead of time. Each of the facilitators took one group through the established circle components: circle opener, circle guidelines, values round question, five discussion round questions, and circle closer. We began the discussion round questions with some personal sharing about what was going on in the lives of the participants. Eventually, we threaded in some middle-level and deep-ended questions. "What has been difficult for you this year?" We asked this question because our school had experienced three administration changes in two years, compounded by a school culture that could be described as struggling, at best. We weren't sure what to expect from the responses to this question, but it turned out to be a great opportunity for everyone to better understand one another and the circumstances that could be causing stress. We added a question about possible solutions. Finally, we brought the participants out of the deep-ended questions and concluded on a very positive note: "Tell us something about you that would surprise all of us." This invitation turned into a humorous round of sharing. All the participants treated one another with respect as they spoke about interesting hobbies, former jobs, and embarrassing yet endearing stories from their past. We wrapped up the circles by simply asking the staff to rate their experience in circle with a Fist-to-Five—rating the experience by flashing a number of fingers. The responses revealed unanimous fours and fives. When I checked in with the other facilitators, they shared similar results with the success of circles and the ratings given at the end.

I noticed two strange phenomena as the faculty meeting wound up. Staff members were smiling and sticking around. Usually after a meeting, a herd of teachers bolted out of the building to the parking lot to head home for the night (sometimes I myself am part of that herd!). I understand why. Many of us have families, workouts, grading papers, or other responsibilities to attend to, and some of us have already put in a 10-hour day. But this time was different. Conversations continued in the hallways—and not among just one group of teachers. I saw multiple groups of four, five, or more teachers talking, laughing, and listening to one another. I saw several pairs of teachers in deep discussion as they stood outside the rooms that had hosted circle. It was a stark difference from the stressed and overwhelmed expressions that I usually saw on my colleagues' faces—and that I exhibited myself. I realized that we, as a staff, needed opportunities like this to listen to one another in a safe environment. We needed to laugh, to share, to understand, and to support one another.

Testimonial from John Whalen

I've experienced so many powerful moments participating in staff or teacher circles. I'd like to share one story from a training in Texas. I have the privilege of working with some amazing people who are part of NEDRP. I traveled to Texas from New York in the summer of 2016 to lend a hand with facilitating some of the trainings. We were working with roughly 100 teachers as part of a two-day overview of what the philosophy of Restorative Practices is; how we interpret it; the proactive (green) structures, reactive (red) structures, and curricular and SEL (yellow) structures of circles; and the mind-set of a restorative practitioner. We also took the trainees through the experience of circle. It's always interesting to watch people as they enter the training. Some are eager to learn about this philosophy. Some realize that they are highly relational and find value in learning new tricks of the trade. Then there are those who are skeptical. They are unsure about this movement and sometimes concerned about the potential loss of the comfort of familiarity offered by traditional philosophies of discipline and classroom management.

    In particular, I noticed that one of the teachers was extremely skeptical of circle. He offered very little comment, and his body language communicated disinterest. His group met with Denise and me (she and I sat in circle together) for two sessions over two days. We slowly saw this teacher participate more as we learned more about each other. By the second circle meeting, he was fully engaged and sharing deeply. The circle moved to very deep and personal sharing, talking about issues including racism and the inequities in education. The whole training group came back together after breaking out into smaller circles, and this participant asked if he could share something. He said that he was amazed at what had happened over the two days and that he had completely shifted his mind-set from what it had been when he entered the training. Then he pointed to a gentleman sitting across from him. He said something like this: "I learned more about this man right here in the last two circles than I have working with him in the same building for the last 10-plus years." I can't remember the exact quote, but that was

The Flexibility of Circles

the essence of it. It was powerful. Here we were, a diverse group of educators sitting in a circle—black, white, Hispanic, and Asian, male and female, administrators and teachers, believers and atheists. In this incredibly diverse environment, circle offered individuals comfort in participation, equitable opportunities to share, to hear different points of view, and to learn about pathways that could build relationships with other people.

I recommend advocating for staff relationship building circles in the school where you work. I've learned things in circle that have fostered personal connections with coworkers that I might not have been able to create without the opportunities offered by circle. Talk to the building administrator about your idea. Volunteer to be a facilitator. Part II, "Circle Scripts," includes three different staff circle scripts that I created and have facilitated with multiple staffs. Faculty meetings are great venues for circling. Beginning-of-the-year kickoff days before the students arrive also offer an ideal chance to set a positive tone in the building where you work. Staff can share what they did over the summer. New teachers get the chance to meet some of their coworkers at a time when creating new relationships can be easier than usual.

I believe that staff circles showcase the power and the value of circle. Embedding circles in the school environment for all stakeholders communicates a central message that relationships and equity are important. Administrators who promote the use of circles thereby relay their significance to the staff.

Yellow Curricular Circles: Pairing Relationship Building with Classroom Content (Circle Scripts 13–15)

Jensen (2009) states that almost half of all secondary students are bored every day, and one of every six high school students is bored in every single class. What do students enjoy the most? Choosing from nine different delivery methods for content (discussion and debate, art and drama activities, group projects, role-playing, presentations, individual reading, research projects, writing projects, and teacher lectures), students said they enjoyed discussion and debate the most. This preference was five or six times greater than the least-enjoyed method: teacher lectures (Jensen 2009, 134). It just so happens that the circle process promotes discussion and respectful debate!

Before we delve into curricular circles, it's important to read the following statement carefully: Not all of your circles should be curricular or content circles! Ideally, these can be sprinkled in from time to time. We go by the theory that at least 75% of circles should be rooted in relationship building. Also, do not start with curricular circles right off the bat. Let your students learn about and get comfortable with the basic structure of circle before you try these. Okay, now back to curricular circles.

I began experimenting with curricular circles a few years ago. We had finished our ratios and proportions unit, concluding with a test on Thursday of that week. I did not want to start the integers unit on a Friday. I also wanted to do a circle with my group. We had done five or six relationship building circles up to that point, and I began brainstorming about how I could introduce some of the concepts of negative numbers that I would be teaching on Monday while creating a discussion that would help us identify class values and strengthen relationships within the class. I came up with the idea that we would have a circle based on positive and negative thinking.

On my blackboard, I drew a giant number line that spanned from -10 to +10. I selected a circle opener that invited students to express how they were feeling by choosing a certain temperature. Warm temperatures (which we value and take full advantage of in upstate New York!) meant that they were feeling good, while colder temperatures meant that they were a bit off. We reviewed our values from the last circle and began with some fun questions to get us sharing.

Then I told a fictitious story about a student whose teacher had asked him to move his seat to the back of the room. Under each person's seat in our circle was a sticky note that was either green or red. I asked the students to brainstorm quietly about how they would have handled the situation. I explained to them that a red note represented a negative thought while a green note represented a positive thought. I asked them to take a minute and come up with an action that a student could take based on the color of the sticky note he or she had received. Once they had completed that task, I passed the talking piece around. Each student shared the color of the sticky note he had found and the thought that he might have had as the student in this situation.

Then we discussed the number line. Students in sixth grade understand the value of positive numbers but are often initially confused when presented with the value of negative numbers. It's strange to them that -1 has a higher value than -10 when +1 has less value than +10. After the students shared what they had written as their thoughts, they had to walk up to the number line one by one and place the sticky note where they expected it to fall along the positive-negative continuum when the possible outcomes of their thoughts were considered. One by one, they followed the instructions. All of the red notes ended up on the negative side of the line, while all of the green notes ended up on the positive side. The follow-up questions asked them to think about possible outcomes if the thoughts led to action. We noted that negative thoughts usually lead to negative outcomes, whereas positive thoughts often lead to an opportunity to repair the conflict with the teacher. It was a great conversation. Just as important, it gave my students a useful introduction to how positive and negative numbers and their values work. It set up perfect prior knowledge for me to tap into on Monday when I began teaching the unit.

Planning curricular circles takes some time, brainstorming, an understanding of what is important to your students, and flexibility. I've had only a few curricular circles be duds. Well-crafted curricular circles relate student experience and interest to a central theme, concept, or main idea that you want to teach. I've witnessed a number of curricular lessons that left the facilitator pleasantly surprised at the conclusion. Teachers express how satisfied they are with student understanding when concepts are presented in a discussion format. The circle also teaches students to listen respectfully to viewpoints that may be different from their own.

Yellow SEL Circles (Circle Scripts 10–12)

I'm a fan of the work of the Collaborative for Academic, Social, and Emotional Learning (CASEL) in identifying the important topics that constitute SEL and in advocating the inclusion of SEL as part of the explicit curriculum (the stated curriculum) rather than the hidden curriculum (the curriculum that is unintentionally taught). CASEL defines social and emotional learning as "the process through which children and adults acquire and effectively apply the knowledge, attitudes, and skills necessary to understand and manage emotions, set and achieve positive goals, feel and show empathy for others, establish and maintain positive relationships, and make responsible decisions" (CASEL 2017). CASEL identifies five core competencies of SEL: self-awareness, self-management, social awareness, relationship skills, and responsible decision-making. Circles can be constructed to address these competencies (see Part II of this book for examples of relevant circle scripts).

I've noticed that some teachers want to focus exclusively on SEL topics (like respect, empathy, responsibility, and so on) for all of their circles. I've also noticed that the result of such a narrow interpretation of circles is that the students lose interest in participating in circles at all. Yes, the circle structure offers the opportunity to discuss SEL topics. However, saying to elementary and even middle school students, "Tell me what respect means to you" can turn circle into a game of "pass the talking piece." Be creative in coming up with questions that get students to talk about situations that involve respect. Build questions that will allow them to call upon their prior knowledge and experiences as a guide to understanding and speaking content. Instead of asking, "What does respect mean to you?" you can lead with something like "Tell us about a time when someone treated you well or nicely." With that kind of open-ended starter, students will hear a number of examples of respect and will begin to build their own knowledge base of what respect means.

Red Reactive Circles (Circle Scripts 16–17)

Circles can be an effective structure for addressing a conflict or issue within a community. Unfortunately, people often think that circles are used exclusively for repairing harm or discussing difficult topics. Many teachers have asked me to come to their classrooms to facilitate a red circle in reaction to their perception that things were not going well. This usually will not work because there likely have not been many opportunities yet for that class to build community through trust and understanding. How do you "restore" what wasn't there in the first place? I advise teachers to invest time in green relationship building circles. Yes, I can come in and facilitate a red circle, but that will likely not get the results that the teacher is hoping for.

Doing solely red circles establishes a dangerous precedent. Participants may begin to regard circle as a punishment. "Oh, no, what did we do wrong this time?" I actually did hear this from a group that I initially circled with because of an issue in their class. I planned to do a green circle when I went to circle with them for the second time. The students had a hard time transitioning to that positive circle because at that point they had experienced circle only as something that occurred after they had made mistakes.

I don't spend a whole lot of time facilitating reactive circles. My limited experience with them has taught me that for those circles to be effective, I need to be very intentional when it comes to the questions I ask. I often ask the participants to reflect on and share how a certain behavior makes them feel and how it may get in the way of their learning. If you are the facilitator, never single out one person in the group. Students sometimes will hold themselves accountable for their actions, which is powerful when it happens. Just don't call them out. Build questions that address the issues. Share ideas on how the community can take steps to improve. As the facilitator, or possibly the teacher of the class in which a red circle happens, participate and let the community know what steps you yourself will take to improve the situation. Write down their suggestions. After the circle is over, it's extremely important to follow up by periodically reviewing the ideas that were shared during the circle discussion. If the community fails to have this opportunity, the probability that authentic change will occur is slim.

CIRCLE MAMMA'S DIARY #6

Let Circle Take Its Course

One of the biggest mistakes you can make as a circle facilitator is to try to fix things in circle. Circle is not about fixing things. It's not about giving advice or answers. It's not about participants giving answers that you are looking for. It's about listening. It's about learning. It's about sharing ourselves and who we are. There may be times when students share something that is uncomfortable to hear. You may hear something inappropriate. Just remember that circle is not about fixing things.

A few years ago I facilitated a circle at a DAEP campus where the teachers were not finding success in circling. They told me that the kids didn't do well in circle and did not want any part of it. I opened the circle by having the group of participants, which included the teachers, listen to a song that my son wrote. The song talks about where we currently are and what our destination is.

Somewhere Out There

By Kameron Holliday

[Hook]

Out there (somewhere)
find my destiny it's out there (somewhere)
tryna find love Out there (somewhere)
searching for a purpose Out there (somewhere)
just a Solivagant hermit Out there (somewhere)
am i crucial am i worthless Out there (somewhere)
am i faultless or deserving Out there (somewhere)
all these answers all these answers Out there (somewhere)

[Verse 1]

Out there somewhere where it's gotta be probably like geometry how it shape your psychology possibly made the prodigy lost in his deep philosophies, god is he, subject to study like he astrology, a star and ever shining his mind working so constantly, but his heart beat been quiet how tom and jerry speak, by the weeks end he's weak willed with his melodies till his feet bleed deep seep down where the devil sleep, and he's feeling like he's sheep how he feed on the life that he live with no will, freedom when he creep with the page and the ink that he spill and retreat when he write to show skill, kid flows so real, pen cold as steel, and never playing games whether deal or no deal, but still he do conceal, the brash thoughts that all just happen to appeal, to the quest i been on lately, all the fresh memories feel distant, it's like the future's here or like i missed it, appealing to your senses but still blinding to your vision, the census try to censor our minds and i'm a witness, so exercise the feeling like it's fitness it's so uplifted, proud that i did this, feeling the calm of the tempest, that's stemming from the abyss of my soul, but i'm still but i'm still tryna figure where i go, was i meant to die young or live old, am i meant to find love or be alone, will i strive or be left with no home, all the answers down the ever forked road, out there somewhere beyond the cold.

After the song, we moved on to the values round and I noticed confusion on the faces of many of the students. When I asked them about it, they told me that the reason for the confusion was that they had never done a values round in any of their circles. The values round went well, and next we turned to the discussion round. I wanted the students to experience a sense of ownership, or belonging, with the circle. I decided to ask the group if anyone had a question that they would like to share. (Before I continue with this account, I should say that I would never recommend this to a teacher who is just learning how to facilitate circle. I've come to trust the circle process wholeheartedly, and I just jumped into it headfirst.)

On this occasion, a student volunteered to ask a question. I passed the talking piece to him and he asked, "What time is it?" One of his teachers spoke out immediately: "See, that's what I'm talking about. They don't want to do this. Get him out of here!" The other adults quickly stood up to begin the process of removing the student from the classroom. I said, "No! Please let him stay here!" Now, I was thinking about his question, and it dawned on me that it could possibly be a very good one. The student who asked the question was holding the talking piece, and he shared first. "It's time for me to get my shit together," he said. He passed the talking piece to the next student. "It's time for my dad to start paying the child support he is supposed to pay my mom." Wow. The next student shared that it was time for him to stop smoking so much marijuana. The talking piece made its way around the circle and the students continued to share.

The Flexibility of Circles

One student even said, "1:30 p.m." I've found that students who give answers like this, meaning responses that seem silly or immature, often do so because they feel like a fish out of water. They are in an environment that they are not used to. They feel like I did as a child. There is a good chance that they are never asked to share their thoughts, feelings, or knowledge with others. So they give responses like this one because they are scared or uncomfortable. If we respond in a corrective or negative way, we relay the wrong message. We end up communicating that there is something wrong with them or their ideas. This could make it even more difficult for them to share when future questions or ideas come up in circle. When we respond by trying to fix them, or their responses, we push them further away. Circle is all about sharing, listening, and learning about each other. It's not a place for judging. In circle, we are all equals. Participants' responses to a question or idea are their own thing, their voices to share. I don't get to judge their responses. They are reading us to see how we are going to react. They are reading us possibly to see if we might be the ones who walk out on them. We need to earn their trust just as much as we want them to trust us.

As the circle with these students continued, they began to trust the process. I felt that the teachers in the class didn't want anything to do with it. Circle exposes you; it's truly who you are. Teachers sometimes don't like to be out there in the open. They may feel vulnerable. Their values and culture may not align with the values and culture of their students. I feel like we make too many assumptions about our kids. We see them with their headphones on. Their pants may be sagging. They communicate differently than we do. We don't get their music. The thing is, we don't know what the words they are listening to mean to them. Sometimes we need to be intentional and take the time to be still and really listen to what they say, what inspires them, and what they stand for.

After the circle, I thought about the question the student asked. "What time is it?" The lyrics of the song, "Somewhere Out There," might have sparked his question. For him, the question meant that he needed to figure out what his next step in life was. What would lead him to his destiny. We need to give participants the opportunity to let the process play out. Facilitators—and teachers, for that matter—often want to try to "fix" situations when they are not comfortable. The teachers wanted to make it about themselves and how they are in control. Facilitators need to remove themselves from the center because circle does not belong to them. Circle belongs to no one.

CHAPTER 7

Tips and Strategies for Facilitating Circle

> Experience is a master teacher, even when it's not our own.
> —*Gina Greenlee,* Postcards and Pearls:
> Life Lessons from Solo Moments on the Road

Experience is key when implementing circles in your classroom. The NEDRP team has learned so much through the hundreds of circles that we have participated in. Teachers usually comment on how well we run circle when we serve as facilitators in their classrooms. There is no magic potion that causes us to be effective facilitators. The real magic, as in almost anything that you try to do that is new, comes through experience. We've learned quite a bit through playing in circle over the years, and we've identified a number of management tips and strategies for you to consider as you look to start facilitating circle. Consider these our best practices!

We've divided this chapter into digestible subsections:
- Planning for Circle
- Arranging and Maintaining the Physical Circle
- Facilitating Circle
- Navigating Difficult Topics/Discussions
- Building a School Culture That Values Circle

Planning for Circle

Intentionally Schedule Circle

This is a big one. Your classroom will learn how to circle and will learn to value circle if it becomes a consistent ritual. Don't expect circle to be very effective if you hold it only two or three times a year. If that's the case, I guarantee that you will spend the majority of your circle time in going over guidelines and managing guidelines. Remember, circle is an investment in creating a positive community based on authentic relationships. Investments made early can pay large dividends down the road.

Make it a point to intentionally schedule circle (or at least some form of relationship building activity) as part of your routine. On the elementary level, consider reserving 20 to 45 minutes a week for circle. Maybe replace one day of morning meeting with circle time. In one fifth-grade class I worked with, we did circle every Friday from 1:30 to about 2:15. This led into the students' earned free time for the week. Circle was a great way to wrap up the week with this group. For middle and high school, the scheduling may be a bit more challenging. It's asking quite a bit to give up an entire class period every week or two. Consider investing two minutes of each class on the two-minute connection strategy that was discussed earlier (p. 65). With that kind of consistency each day, participants will get used to sharing with one another. After four or five weeks, introduce the students to circle. Tell them that circle is just like the two-minute connection. The main differences are that the talking piece is used, everyone is sitting in a circle, and there is a centerpiece.

Your First Circle Will Probably Not Go as Planned!

That's the truth. Recall the story that I told in Chapter 1 about my first attempt at circle? It was a disaster. Now look at me. I'm writing a book on how valuable the process is! I did not give up on circle. The first few attempts did not go as planned, but I kept trying. I kept modeling expectations, I stopped circle if the talking piece was "disrespected," I complimented our group when we did great, and I influenced our community to do better when we were struggling. I used scripts that I found in the first book I bought. Not only will your first circle probably not go as planned, but you may have the same outcome for your second and third circles. It takes time for students to "learn" circle. It takes us, as facilitators, time to "learn" circle. Do not feel like you are failing if circle doesn't go well the first time. This is normal!

Circle Should Not Be Used Solely as a Reactive Intervention

Many teachers get the impression that circle will "fix" their class or resolve a major issue that is bringing a community of learners down. As noted earlier (p. 74), reactive circles work well when relationships have already been established in the classroom. However, most of the teachers who have asked me to facilitate such circles have invested little or no time in first creating opportunities for their classes to meet proactively in relationship building circles.

In some settings I've seen students associate circle with being in trouble as a group. They may show irritation when they see that a circle has been set up. They say, "Oh, we're in trouble" or "What did we do?" Such a negative orientation can derail the entire concept of circle for a classroom and even for a whole school. In contrast, students in schools that invest in relationship building circles are likely to get excited when they see the seats set in a circle with a centerpiece in the middle. Our belief is that such commitment at the outset results in fewer situations that would require a red circle. Classrooms that have invested in relationship building circles and at some point later need repair have a much better chance that a reactive circle will be effective, since the community will know what the expectations are for circle and hopefully will have already made genuine efforts to build an environment that supports open and honest sharing. Remember, you have to CONNECT with your students before you have the opportunity to CORRECT your students.

Move into Curricular Circles and SEL Circles Only after Establishing Solid Relationships in the Group

Our workshop participants are always intrigued by the idea of implementing curricular circles in their classrooms, and for good reason. Circle offers a dynamic structure for learning and teaching. Teachers new to the practice want to jump right in and try curricular circles immediately. These teachers usually wind up struggling, however, because they have not spent sufficient time in developing an understanding of the fundamental expectations and guidelines of circle before trying to use it for teaching. They can become so frustrated by the difficulties they experience by starting with curricular circles that they end up abandoning the entire process without giving it an honest shot. Relationship building circles as a starting point are great not only for developing strong relationships within the group but also for teaching the fundamental "how" of circle.

I suggest that circle should focus mostly on relationship building, though curricular and SEL circles can certainly yield dynamic meetings. I use a ratio of 3:1 for the types of circles I conduct; that is, I attempt to do three relationship building circles for every curricular or SEL circle.

Be Consistent: Implement the Components of Circle When Planning

Make circle a ritual and maintain the established structure. Include a circle opener and a circle closer and explicitly announce each. These may be very brief parts of your overall circle, but don't discount them. Some of the ideas for opening and closing circles that I share in the "Circle Building Tools" section (Part III) use a quote, a poem, a "thumbs-up" or "thumbs-down," or even have circle participants share quickly with whoever they are sitting next to. A yoga stretch or other type of movement activity can also serve as an effective but brief circle closer.

Sometimes I have skipped the values round because I felt that I wouldn't have enough time for my circle. I've learned, however, that the values round is one of the best ways to develop mutual respect and build community. Not every values round has to involve writing something on a paper plate. Sometimes we set out the plates that we created when we shared what traits we admired with someone we know (I almost always start a new group with this question. They write the quality on paper plates and we create another circle with the plates around the centerpiece.) Then I'll use a review of the qualities on the plates as the values round instead of doing an activity or answering a question. Values rounds can be implemented quickly also, if necessary. Just make sure that you do provide time in future circles to continue building upon group values. It's really important!

Use Student Input for Creating Circle Questions

Sometimes we just need to ask students directly to share what is on their minds. There are many ways to structure that question. The two-minute connection is one effective strategy. Other ways to discover important issues that participants are wrestling with include administering interest inventories, providing opportunities for students to write freely, encouraging them to keep journals, and pursuing conversations with them outside of the classroom setting.

An activity that has been successful for me is that I write 20 random questions on the board and randomly select students to choose one of the questions to be used in circle. Students enjoy doing this and will often pick questions that they are interested in. My advisory group a few years back was so enthusiastic about this activity that we made it a weekly ritual.

Circle Does Not Substitute for Classroom Management

If anything, circle will either confirm or expose whether a teacher can manage a classroom effectively. The best circle facilitators are consistent, patient, caring, organized, able to listen, and able to share (as well as possessing many other laudatory qualities). Good classroom managers also exhibit these qualities. However, circle is not a classroom management program. Circle won't fix your classroom in 10 days. Circle is not baptismal water that instantly heals our struggling classes and communities. Many people harbor this misconception. They view it as a silver bullet. But there are no silver bullets, folks! Circle gives you a structure through which you can initiate healthy relationships, talk about important topics, and create opportunities for respect to grow among people who spend a great deal of time together.

The trick to persuading students to abide by classroom rules is to build an authentic relationship with them. Think about a student who struggles in a number of classrooms but is successful in some others. I would guess that a positive relationship has been built between student and teacher in the classrooms where the student experiences success.

Trouble Building Your Circle? Try Some of Our Scripts

Part II of this book includes multiple circle scripts. Consider trying these scripts if you are a teacher or facilitator who finds it difficult to come up with ideas for your own circle. Make the suggested scripts your own. Pick and choose among them and then add more as your comfort with the process increases. Part III offers many tools for creating circle content.

Arranging and Maintaining the Physical Circle

Model That Talking Piece!

The talking piece is the great equalizer. It gives students a fair opportunity to be heard. Students and adults will struggle with the talking piece at first. This is especially true in more talkative classrooms. It takes some time to teach the talking piece procedure. The best way to do so is for the facilitator to model its use. Start with some light questions, like "What month is your birthday?" Pass the talking piece around the circle until it gets back to you. Then ask the group to describe how you acted. Ask them if you did a good job of following the talking piece guidelines. Have the class reflect on how they did with the talking piece by going around the circle again and using a strategy like Fist-to-Five.

We teachers have a hard time taking that teacher hat off in general and certainly in circle. I once observed a relationship building circle in which the facilitator asked a question, passed the talking piece to the next person, and then proceeded to comment immediately (without the talking piece!) on each reply. That was not circle! Circle is not 10 or 20 different one-on-one conversations. That facilitator dominated the circle by overvaluing his own voice. All equity was lost in this situation. The students mostly tuned out and became disinterested. We want the participants to feel **and** be as important as the facilitator. As facilitator, ask the question, answer only when it's your turn, and watch circle happen!

Utilize Nonverbal Cues with the Talking Piece

Students can get excited when other students share something that is meaningful to them, and often the listeners have a hard time remaining quiet themselves. In the midst of their enthusiasm they tend to yell out their comments and questions. This is a very natural response. Many adults do the same thing when in conversation with one another. Such engagement in the discussion, while positive, does lead to people speaking without the talking piece, however, which can easily overwhelm what might otherwise be a productive discussion. It might take a while for students who are new to circle to really get why we need to use a talking piece. I've often had new teachers who are attempting to facilitate circle look at me helplessly in such a situation.

We've developed some strategies that have been effective in helping students respect the use of the talking piece. I've found that simply placing my index finger over my lips gives students a quiet reminder of what their responsibilities are. I only ever interrupt circle as a facilitator if the talking piece is being blatantly ignored by a few participants. Even in this situation, I may stand up, walk over to the person who has the talking piece, and ask for it. Then I can speak to the class about our expectations. As always, I try to use affective statements (I-statements) to tell them how the violation of the talking piece is making me feel instead of singling out students who are having a hard time with using the talking piece properly.

We model thumbs-up to our participants every time we meet in circle. We ask students to give a thumbs-up if they like or love what another person says. If they REALLY love what another student says they can give two thumbs-up. As the facilitator, I intentionally model this as students share. I'll make eye contact with students who may be about to say something out of excitement and flash a thumbs-up at them. I may remind a group that struggled during a specific question that we need to use our thumbs to communicate. (We suggest that you discourage the use of thumbs-down in circle. The reason? We want to build relationships rooted in respect. Does flashing thumbs-down at what participants share promote respect?)

We also use other nonverbal clues. I have a "love it" gesture that I model for my students. If they say something that touches me deeply, I make a fist with one hand, place it over my heart, and tap gently once or twice. And my students taught me a way to communicate "me too!" nonverbally: Point to your chest with the thumb of one hand, then point away from your body with the pinkie finger of that hand.

Select Your Talking Piece Logically

Be creative when choosing a talking piece, aiming to select something that you think will be meaningful for your group. Keep in mind that the talking piece itself can become something you'll need to manage in circle. Earlier I spoke about my bamboo talking piece and how it is my go-to choice for most of the circles that I facilitate. That piece doesn't work well with younger students, though, because it could hurt them. Think about safety when choosing what to use.

Also, consider whether the talking piece you want to use might become a distraction. Once I watched a facilitator use a bell as a talking piece with a group of fifth graders. The students were captivated by the sound of the bell ringing, and many chose to ring it while sharing, which led to laughter but unfortunately inattention as well. Another facilitator whose group I observed used a battery-powered professional wrestling microphone as a talking piece for adult staff circles. It was fun to watch each participant hold the microphone and talk into it while sharing, and this led to many respectful chuckles. The microphone had a button that imitated crowd noise and the match bell ringing. When I heard that I instantly thought about how it would lead to distraction if it were used by students in circle.

I've seen all sorts of talking pieces, among them sunglasses, rolled-up paper, flowers, foam hammers, sentimental pieces. Be careful, though, if you decide to use a framed image (think 4" x 6" or so); the talking piece ends up being dropped quite a bit, and in this case broken glass might be an unwelcome outcome of circle! And a final, probably obvious, tip: Be sure that your talking piece is not an item that has significant monetary or sentimental value.

Keep Your Centerpiece Fresh

Participants value circle centerpieces. Well-conceived centerpieces can serve as tools for teaching more about the facilitator, the participants, the community, and the topic being discussed. I try to switch up what I add to the circle centerpiece when I meet with the same group multiple times, bringing in new items that tell more about me. I have found, for example, that participants love photos of my family as well as pictures of me doing some of my favorite things. It's also more than fine to reuse pieces. I often select the same basic pieces for the first few meetings with a new group and then add to those. I've noticed that as we meet more often, participants want to learn more about me. Many surprising and constructive connections can be made when participants find a relational pathway from one of the pieces you share. And you can make more connections with more pieces!

Tips and Strategies for Facilitating Circle

An illustration: I found that students became really engaged when I shared about time that I spent with other teachers. I go on an annual winter backpacking trip with one of my coworkers. After our return, my students were so interested in what we did on our trip that on circle day and beyond, many of them came up to me and asked great questions about our experience. I also shared a picture of our staff coed soccer team. Many of our students had no clue that their teachers played on an athletic team together. Once they found out, we had to give them updates every Wednesday morning during the season on the outcome of the game and who scored goals or contributed assists. (I was the goalie and never got mentioned! Talk about equity!)

Promote Student Involvement in Creating Talking Piece and Centerpiece

Sometimes we forget how important our circle participants are. We use our talking pieces and our centerpieces and facilitate, facilitate, facilitate. To depart from that habit a bit, consider asking a student to bring in something to be used for the next talking piece. Have her explain why the piece is important. It's a surefire way to learn more about that student. A variation on that idea is to offer objects that are part of the centerpiece as talking pieces. Allow students to pick one that reminds them of something they like or one that symbolizes something important to them. Just make sure that the centerpiece includes items that would also be appropriate as talking pieces.

Students will value being able to add their own contributions to the centerpiece. One classroom I worked with did an excellent job with this, and it proved to be very manageable. I asked the students to bring something for circle that would fit inside a sandwich bag and could be kept at school. They responded with pictures, trinkets, and other items that told their story. Just make sure to communicate expectations and guidelines for this to parents.

Try to Keep Students from Sitting at Desks

Make circle special! Students are used to sitting at desks or tables all day. Think about letting them sit on top of their desks instead (if they are the larger desks). I add this tip because I notice that students (especially elementary students) tend to fidget with things inside their desks while circle is going on. I'm a fidgeter myself, so I get it! However, fidgeting can be a distraction and can lead students to miss important chances to learn more about their peers. Remember, in a perfect world, the students will be sitting in chairs, in a circle, with no obstructions. When that perfection is not possible, try your best to create a different kind of unique setting.

Sit like Your Kids Sit

This great suggestion came from another district coordinator. If everyone is in chairs, the facilitator should also be in a chair. If participants are sitting on the floor, then the facilitator should sit on the floor. Mirroring participants' seating helps the teacher or facilitator to establish a connection with them.

Facilitating Circle

Always Review the Circle Guidelines

Many beginning teachers ask how often they should review circle guidelines with each group. The answer is simple: every time they do circle! Reminding participants about circle guidelines is a very effective proactive measure for managing circle. Review each guideline and ask the class to give you a thumbs-up or a thumbs-down to show whether or not they will agree to follow that guideline.

Another reinforcing technique is making a circle guidelines poster to be placed in a highly visible spot in the classroom. Students will tend to look at it when their minds wander (I was an expert mind wanderer when I was in school!), and consistent review of these guidelines will yield better chances for circle success. You can even have students say the guidelines out loud with you as you review them.

Start with Simple Questions in the Discussion Round

Earlier in this book, we talked about different types of questions: shallow-ended questions, middle-level questions, and deep-ended questions. Some teachers want to jump immediately to asking deep-ended questions—which usually elicit a round of "talking piece hot potato," in which the talking piece is passed quickly around the circle with responses of "Pass!" Be strategic in how you start circle. Start with a simple relationship building question, a shallow-ended question. Students tend to be quite comfortable with questions at this level, so it's a good place to start. When you see that most of the class is participating, you'll be able to assess how they are doing with the talking piece.

Employ Proactive Praise

Students and adults do struggle with the talking piece, especially at first. Proactive praise is very effective in building confidence with it. We've noted that beginning with a shallow-ended question increases the chances of getting off to a good start in the discussion round, so let's say that the group did an excellent job of respecting the talking piece when responding to that easy question. That success gives you an opportunity to praise and show appreciation to the group. Some of my "go-to" comments in such a situation are:

"You guys did a fantastic job with the talking piece!"
"I know it's difficult, but you did it!"
"I'm so appreciative that we are all showing respect to each other. Thank you."

That praise will carry you into the next questions. Students love positive affirmation as much as we adults do. In fact, it may be my most important strategy for managing circle. It just works!

Consider How to Approach Continual Speaking without the Talking Piece

Sometimes, a class is just worked up. The time of day, the day of the week, the dynamic of the class—all or any one of these (and other) factors can result in an "excited" or "talkative" community. The first thing I learned was to be a model of proper participation in circle. I'll try to let responses to a question in the discussion round complete their journey around the circle if there are minimal or few violations of the talking piece along the way. I'll remind the community that we all agreed to try our best to respect the talking piece. I may even review the guidelines for the talking piece again and ask them to give me another thumbs-up for affirmation. I'll explain that I understand that the talking piece guideline is difficult to follow at times. I'll review the silent cues. I'll ask if there are any students who feel like they can't continue in circle, and if there are, I'll offer them a spot outside the circle where they can sit quietly without feeling like they are "in trouble."

I have chosen to pause circle if a number of students are speaking without the talking piece. However, I resort to this only after trying to be as proactive as possible. I might quietly walk over to the person who is speaking and attempt to let that person finish. Then I'll announce that I have to interrupt the circle because we are failing to meet the guidelines that we established as a group. I address the community by using affective "I-statements" similar to those below:

"I am feeling frustrated about how circle is going right now."
"I am having a hard time understanding why people are talking without the talking piece after we all agreed to try our best to respect it."
"I am feeling distracted by the talking that is going on without the talking

piece. I feel that because of this I can't be respectful to those who are sharing."

"I am so sorry that some of you are not being given the opportunity to share as we agreed. It's not fair to you, and I want you to know that I'm trying my best to be respectful of everyone."

I've found this approach to be extremely effective. I depersonalize the situation by using the "I-statements," and thus students don't feel singled out. After circle I usually make an effort to talk privately to individual students about the issues that came up in circle. I use the kind of open-ended questions that we use when addressing conflict between two people.

"What happened today?"
"What were you thinking when it happened?"
"Who was affected by what happened in circle today?"
"How can we make it right with everyone who was affected?"
"What are your needs in this situation and how can I accommodate those needs?"

Using these questions is a great way to address any type of conflict in the classroom, including issues with circle. I do recall one time when I had a student who I believed was intentionally trying to sabotage circle. I tried as many proactive interventions as possible, but none worked, so I finally asked the student to sit outside of the circle. I let the student know that a welcome back to the circle was available upon agreement to follow the guidelines that we had adopted as a group. The student chose not to come back to circle for that meeting. We spoke privately after circle and got back on the same page about what was needed from both of us. This student was successful in all of the future circles that we did that year.

Avoid Questions That Can Easily Be Answered with "Yes" or "No"

In preparation for facilitating a small-group relationship circle, I had brought in a few adults to participate and witness how such circles work. I asked the question "Have you ever lived outside of our city before?" I was hoping that students who had lived outside of the city would share with the rest of us where they had lived. Unfortunately, just about every student simply said either "Yes" or "No" and then passed the talking piece. One participant in the circle suggested that I rephrase the question so that a "yes" or "no" response would not work as an answer. I then changed my statement to, "Share with us the names of the towns or cities where you have lived." The responses for this version were much more descriptive. The only exception to this tip would be for Step-In Circles, which are driven by "yes/no" and "true/false" questions.

Don't Use Circle to Evaluate Student Responses

Circle is not a time to evaluate a student's response to a question. Facilitators should not coach a student through a question. Circle is not an assignment! Teachers should not be judging or grading responses or participation. Use a different structure if you want to evaluate answers to questions or participation in the group.

Don't Assume That the Teacher Always Has to Be the Facilitator

We strongly advise that the teacher serve as the circle facilitator until the community fully embraces the guidelines and format of circle. This acceptance will occur as the community gains experience through participation in a number of circles. Once the group has reached this comfort level with circle, it's fine to branch out to variations of doing circle. For example, invite students to facilitate circle. The assumption of the facilitator role provides them with a significant opportunity to experiment with leadership. Be equitable in assigning the facilitation role. Consider choosing participants at random. You could even have multiple facilitators for a single circle session, assigning a different student for each component of circle. Circle becomes very powerful when the facilitator role can be handed over to any of the participants.

Share Deeply: Students Will Follow Your Lead

I've had some teachers come to me and tell me that they were having difficulty getting students to open up and share. I ask these teachers if they are opening up to the class themselves. I ask them to be intentional about sharing deeply and then see where circle goes. I've found that I've sometimes had new groups share deeply on our first meeting in circle if I was the one stepping in the deep end or the middle end first. Many students will follow your lead, if you are comfortable enough to share deeply.

   A quick note on this: Some students need more time to develop trust in circle than others do. They may not share much at first. This is absolutely understandable, and I'm certain you'll find a student or two in each group that will be more reticent than others. They will move into circle at their own pace and will eventually grow into being able to share deeply.

Model Talking to the Entire Circle, Not Just to One Person

Students oftentimes want to address their comments to the facilitator when it is their turn to share with the group. It's what they are used to doing in most classroom settings when they speak. If the facilitator avoids eye contact with the student, however, that may help him or her find it easier to speak to the whole group. Model this idea to your community when you introduce circle, and review as needed.

Create a Space for Students Who Choose Not to Participate

Remember, circle should always be a voluntary process. Occasionally, though, students will choose not to participate in circle. I've found that arranging for a few quiet places for these students to sit has been most useful for me as a facilitator. I know that some teachers have a difficult time with the idea of allowing some to absent themselves from the class activity, but if those who choose not to participate do have access to a quiet spot, they most likely will still be listening to what is going on in circle. Creating an alternative assignment for the student to work on could be another strategy for this situation.

Some of Your Questions Will Turn Out to Be Duds. Revise, Revise, Revise!

These are the questions that become "talking piece hot potatoes!" Don't take it personally if you have a question that leads to a majority of students passing. Instead, think about how you can change the question in a way that will give students a better chance to feel comfortable sharing an answer. I find that curricular-based questions can often become duds. Think carefully about how you can associate what students already know (prior knowledge) or value (student interest) with the concept or theme that you want them to discuss.

Be Flexible and Don't Force Yourself to Stay on Script

Like lesson plans, circle scripts can be very helpful in guiding a facilitator through circle. When I began teaching, I would try to follow my lesson plans verbatim. This devotion to the lesson plans resulted in some clunky lessons! Sometimes I just expanded on a concept or idea if the students were intrigued. Other times, there were the inevitable opportunities for teachable moments based on what came up in discussion. This happens in circle as well. Be willing to go off script if circle takes you to an unexpected place. Sometimes I would attempt the same circle with five different classes during the same day and would end up having five entirely different experiences.

With regard to time, in circle planning as in lesson planning, it's good to have alternate options in mind in case you wind up with more or less time than you thought you would. I have a few books of questions that I place in my centerpiece for every circle I facilitate. If circle ends early, I can go to some of the questions that are offered by these books. Part III of this book includes question banks that you may find useful. In fact, this book could work as an object in your centerpiece. I try to plan two different circle closers that could work when time allows. I may choose to have a group play "21" if more than five minutes are left, or I may read a poem to the group if only a minute or so remains when I get to the circle closer.

Allow Every Student to Start with a Clean Slate

All of us are sometimes guilty of holding a grudge toward someone who has disrespected us. In the classroom, this can be the student who was rude or the student who vandalized something in our environment. We have to remind ourselves that these students are still children regardless of grade level. Their brains have not fully matured yet. They need to be able to trust us and to feel that we will look past the mistakes that they have made. I've learned—and it took a lot of mistakes for me to do so—that I need to grant students a clean slate after an incident. I treat them with respect, affirm my love and care for them, and strive to make them feel welcome to the learning environment. We want to teach our kids forgiveness, true? What better way for them to learn than through our modeling of this skill.

A quick side note, it you will: I've facilitated countless Restorative Practices conferences with students and teachers following some form of conflict between the two. I pre-conference with both the teacher and the student before bringing them together. I've found that in many, many situations, the student wants to move on and will accept accountability for his or her part in the conflict. However, students are afraid of how the teacher will treat them upon their return to class. They are worried about the "label" they may have earned as a result of the conflict. Granting students a clean slate after an incident is a very effective way to show that you care about them and understand them. Listening to their responses in circle with unwavering attention may allow you to gain a better understanding of them and of why the conflict happened in the first place.

Navigating Difficult Topics/Discussions

Acknowledge Students' Bravery for Deep Sharing

Sometimes a student will share very deeply with the circle. It takes great courage to take this risk. I almost always acknowledge the student's bravery when he or she shares something very personal. This may help other students share more openly while valuing the student who shared deeply. I'll often try to thank someone for sharing deeply when I see that person outside of circle. This usually happens in places like the playground, the hallway, and the cafeteria.

Visit the Deep End, but Don't End There

Circle can sometimes go there. It can get really deep. I've had students share about extremely difficult situations that they are encountering in their lives. Many of the things that they share are challenges that I myself have not experienced. I find it an honor when a student trusts the circles that I facilitate enough to share deeply. I just don't want to end there. I always try to bring us out of the deep end by the time circle is over. Asking a question about something the class is excited about, celebrating a victory for the week, or just sharing something funny can help the group transition from the deep end to a more comfortable place.

Building a School Culture That Values Circle

A Community of Sharing: Share Scripts

Consider putting together a school binder for circle scripts. Develop a specific format or "look" for the scripts so they can be easily identified. A school could assemble quite a collection if each teacher contributed scripts for three circles over the course of a school year.

Invite Guests to Participate in Circle

This is an excellent idea for schools that are just beginning to implement circles. Invite district administrators in for circle. These are the leaders who often drive district policy. Let them experience the power of circle for themselves. Invite building administrators in for circle. This will give building leaders an opportunity to get to know the students of their school in a fantastic way.

Promote the Use of Circle with Staff

Staff circles can become powerful meetings that give groups the opportunity to get to know each other a lot better. Let's be honest—much of the content transmitted in faculty meetings could just as easily be transmitted via e-mail. Supporting a staff that circles will likely lead to a school that embraces circling in its classrooms and reaps the benefits of it through every aspect of the school culture.

CIRCLE MAMMA'S DIARY #7

My Why—Healing Hearts, One Circle at a Time

I shared a little bit of my childhood with you at the beginning of this book. I didn't have the best culture in my home growing up. After my father left, my mom did the best she could. I loved my mother, and I knew that she loved me, yet I didn't feel like I heard that from her very often. There were times when I wished she could have been around more so she could offer me more guidance. As I entered adulthood, I carried with me many of the difficulties that I had felt as a child. I turned into a hardened person. I had trouble trusting people. It was hard for me to show and give love. I've made some mistakes in my life. Those mistakes, along with the traumas I experienced, stuck to me like the clothes I wore each day.

The first circle I ever facilitated was with my family, as I discussed earlier in the book. It helped transform each of us who was involved. I felt that the conflict between my son and his father could have been strained forever. The circle gave each of us, myself included, the opportunity to hear my son's voice. We had the opportunity to hear his father's voice. I really believe that this moment helped build the strong voice that resides within my son. I was overwhelmed with what circle helped us achieve as a family.

Circle helped me to learn that I needed to forgive myself for the mistakes I had made in my life. It also helped me learn to forgive others, including my parents, and it helped my parents forgive me for any pain I may have caused them. We have a wonderful relationship today. Circle has taught me to share myself and my experiences with other people. By doing this, I've been able to release some of the difficult pieces of my life. This made me whole again. It made me believe in the human race. It allowed me the opportunity to trust. Circle taught me to see and understand empathy at a genuine level. I knew this because my heart began to feel emotions when I heard from others. Circle has allowed me to love again. I've been able to peel away the layers of me that were holding me back. I've been able to take down the wall, brick by brick, that I had put up around me for so many years. Circle has been the force that has helped self-transformation occur for me. I got to truly work on me, and for once I took the time to do that. It felt almost selfish, yet knowing where I am at now, I can see that it led to selflessness. Circle has become a way of living for me. I've become a more complete and stronger person than I have ever been. I was able to feel those good things that I felt following so many of my experiences in circle. I've become a better daughter. I've become a better mother. I finally regained my voice, and no one will ever take that from me again. I never want to lose these feelings.

For the children and my students, I want to give them what I needed as a child. I want to give them an opportunity to have their voices heard. I want them to learn about one another more than academically. I want them to be noticed, to feel like they are part of an environment that understands and values them. Think of the students in a class as a group of puzzle pieces. Those who have experienced trauma and pain have many tiny pieces that go into the puzzle. The bigger pieces, the more connected pieces, may represent the people who have not experienced as much pain and trauma. Sitting in circle is like trying to put all of those different-sized pieces together. Wholeness. Connection. Understanding. Empathy. Respect. I want everyone to be given the tools to become whole again, just like I experienced. I want everyone to be noticed and to feel like they are an irreplaceable piece of an amazing whole.

We all have our own dictionaries that we have created to define for us what life is. The dictionary that I had earlier in my life was so different from the one I have now! I've rewritten that old one. My dictionary now has helped me define and understand what true connections are. It has defined what a true relationship is. It defines empathy and true love. It has taught me to define needs and to recognize the needs of other people. Our dictionaries can be rewritten. Some of our students have dictionaries that are like mine was when I was younger. Some of these babies have even worse dictionaries than I had. I just want all the people I come in contact with, whether student, teacher, neighbor, family member, or anybody else, to be able to look at their dictionary and grow as a person.

I can only imagine what circle could have done for me when I was a child in school. I can't go back in time to see what it would have been like, but I can bring circle to our kids today. This is why circle has become a central part of my life. It helped to heal my heart. I know it will give others the chance to heal and grow, one circle at a time.

PART II

Circle Scripts

1. Green GTKY (Getting to Know You) Relationship Building Circle #1 for Grades K–2: Introducing Circle

Circle Time for Grades K–2: 15 to 20 minutes

Circle Opener *(You can use a quote, poem, activity, etc.)*
The Quietest Sound: Tell students that the whole group is going to see how long they can hear the voice of a bell. Have them raise their hands and close their eyes. After they first hear the bell, they should slowly lower their hands as the sound of the bell fades, finally bringing their hands to rest in their laps when they can no longer hear it.

Circle Guidelines *(Review norms of circle, explain talking piece and centerpiece)*
1. Respect the talking piece. You may pass it if you choose to. (Ask for thumbs-up as you state guidelines 1–3. Students who refuse to comply with the guidelines can sit outside of the circle. These instructions apply to all classroom circles.)
2. What is said in circle stays in circle.
3. Safety: If you share something that makes me think your safety is in danger, I must report it by law (mandated reporting).
4. Speak from the heart!

Values Round *(A question or activity that will emphasize the values of those in circle)*
Practice using the talking piece.

Discussion Round *(Questions that you can ask during circle)*
1. Conversation Cubes (Conversation Cubes are dice with questions printed on all sides. To use in circle, roll one of the dice and ask the question that comes up.)
2. In my family we all like to . . .
3. One thing I love about school is . . .
4. Continue with Conversation Cube questions if time allows.

Circle Closer *(Close circle with a quote, poem, activity, question, etc.)*
Compliment Toss: Have all the circle participants stand. Toss a soft ball to one of them and pay that student a compliment. Ask him or her to thank you for the compliment. Then you sit down. The student with the ball calls out

another student's name, gives a compliment, tosses the ball to that person, and then sits down. This continues until only one student is standing. This special student can pick ANY student to receive the compliment.

2. Green GTKY Circle #2 for Grades K–2

Circle Time for Grades K–2: 15 to 20 minutes

Circle Opener *(You can use a quote, poem, activity, etc.)*
On Your Feet! Students stand up if they can answer "yes" to a statement that is made by someone in the circle. Use the talking piece to have someone make the statement. Pass the talking piece around the circle to allow everyone an opportunity to speak.

Circle Guidelines *(Review norms of circle, explain talking piece and centerpiece)*
1. Respect the talking piece. You may pass it if you choose to.
2. What is said in circle stays in circle.
3. Safety (mandated reporting)
4. Speak from the heart!

Values Round *(A question or activity that will emphasize the values of those in circle)*
Practice using the talking piece.

Discussion Round *(Questions that you can ask during circle)*
1. Conversation Cubes
2. What is your favorite green thing?
3. What's one thing that you wish you knew how to do?
4. I am very good at . . .
5. Continue with Conversation Cubes if time allows.

Circle Closer *(Close circle with a quote, poem, activity, question, etc.)*
It's All Mime! Students mime certain feelings based on situations described by the facilitator. Examples: How would you look if you slammed your finger in a door? If you lost your bike? If your friend found your bike? If your favorite song came on the radio? If you had to try a food that you didn't like? If you heard a really loud sound? If you scraped your knee on the blacktop?

3. Green GTKY Circle #3 for Grades K–2

Circle Time for Grades K–2: 20 to 30 minutes

Circle Opener *(You can use a quote, poem, activity, etc.)*
All Change: The students stand in a circle, and the teacher taps one on the shoulder. That person starts an action (e.g., clapping), which the others have to follow. The teacher taps another student on the shoulder, and the group changes to a new action selected by that student.

Circle Guidelines *(Review norms of circle, explain talking piece and centerpiece)*
1. Respect the talking piece. You may pass it if you choose to.
2. What is said in circle stays in circle.
3. Safety (mandated reporting)
4. Speak from the heart!

Values Round *(A question or activity that will emphasize the values of those in circle)*
Practice using the talking piece.
My favorite color is . . .
The best thing about a friend is . . .

Discussion Round *(Questions that you can ask during circle)*
1. Conversation Cubes x 2 (roll dice twice for two questions)
2. When I grow up, I want to . . .
3. I get mad when . . .
4. What is the best gift that you have ever received?
5. Tell us something that your teacher does really well.

Circle Closer *(Close circle with a quote, poem, activity, question, etc.)*
The Quietest Sound: Tell students that the whole group is going to see how long they can hear the voice of a bell. Have them raise their hands and close their eyes. After they first hear the bell, they should slowly lower their hands as the sound of the bell fades, finally bringing their hands to rest in their laps when they can no longer hear it.

4. Green GTKY Circle #1 for Grades 3–6: Introducing Circle

Circle Opener *(You can use a quote, poem, activity, etc.)*
Let's root for each other and watch each other grow!
(There is a great image of this quote in Google Images. It would be a nice addition to any centerpiece.)

Circle Guidelines *(Review norms of circle, explain talking piece and centerpiece)*
1. Respect the talking piece. You may pass it if you choose to.
2. What is said in circle stays in circle.
3. Safety (mandated reporting)
4. Speak from the heart!

Values Round *(A question or activity that will emphasize the values of those in circle)*
Plate Activity: Give each participant in the circle a paper plate. Have each person write down the name of someone who is important to him or her along with one thing to admire about the person. Once everyone has finished, place the paper plates inside the circle. You can simply push the plates toward the center of the circle or you can use them to make a circle that surrounds the centerpiece.

Discussion Round *(Questions that you can ask during circle)*
1. Conversation Cubes x 2
2. If you could travel anywhere in the world, where would you go? Who would you take with you?
3. Name one thing that you would like to have in the future.
4. What's the hardest thing for you to do?
5. If you had a magic wand, what would you do with it?
6. What has been the best thing about __th grade so far?
7. What is one thing that you learned about someone in circle today?

Circle Closer *(Close circle with a quote, poem, activity, question, etc.)*
Students will play either of the following games, depending on available time:
Count to 10: Students work together as a group to count to 10. There is one twist: Only one person can say one number at a time. If more than one person says the next number, the counting must start over at 1. The facilitator keeps track of how many attempts it takes.

Circle Scripts

"21": Students can say up to three numbers at a time. Count in order until someone has to say "21." That person is eliminated from the game. The class in unison says "good morning" or "good afternoon" to the student who has been eliminated. Restart each round at 1 and play until only one person remains.

5. Green GTKY Circle #2 for Grades 3–6

Circle Opener *(You can use a quote, poem, activity, etc.)*
My Weekend: Tell us one thing about your weekend.

Circle Guidelines *(Review norms of circle, explain talking piece and centerpiece)*
1. Respect the talking piece. You may pass it if you choose to.
2. What is said in circle stays in circle.
3. Safety (mandated reporting)
4. Speak from the heart!

Values Round *(A question or activity that will emphasize the values of those in circle)*
What makes a good friend?

Discussion Round *(Questions that you can ask during circle)*
1. Conversation Cubes x 2
2. What is your favorite app or game?
3. If you could own the world's largest collection of something, what would it be?
4. Who do you wish would listen more closely to you?
5. What has been the most challenging part of ____th grade?
6. If you could choose whether to be rich, happy, or famous, which one would you pick?

Circle Closer *(Close circle with a quote, poem, activity, question, etc.)*
Compliment Toss: Have all the circle participants stand. Toss a soft ball to a participant and pay that person a compliment. Ask the participant to thank you for the compliment. Then you sit down. The student with the ball calls out another student's name, gives a compliment, tosses the ball to the student, and then sits down. This continues until only one student is standing. This special student can pick ANY student to receive the compliment.

6. Green GTKY Circle #3 for Grades 3–6

Circle Opener *(You can use a quote, poem, activity, etc.)*
The best way to predict your future is to create it.   —*Abraham Lincoln*

Education is the passport to the future, for tomorrow belongs to those that prepare for it today.   —*Malcolm X*

Leadership is about making others better as a result of your presence and making sure that impact lasts in your absence.   —*Sheryl Sandberg*

Education is the most powerful weapon which you can use to change the world.   —*Nelson Mandela*

Circle Guidelines *(Review norms of circle, explain talking piece and centerpiece)*
1. Respect the talking piece. You may pass it if you choose to.
2. What is said in circle stays in circle.
3. Safety (mandated reporting)
4. Speak from the heart!

Values Round *(A question or activity that will emphasize the values of those in circle)*
What is the most important quality for a leader to have?

Discussion Round *(Questions that you can ask during circle)*
1. Conversation Cubes
2. If you could have an unlimited gift card to any one restaurant, which one would you choose?
3. If you could change one thing about yourself, what would you change?
4. If you could send a text message to every person in the world, what would it say?
5. What would you like to be doing in 15 years?
6. What is one thing you need to focus on that will help you achieve this goal?

Circle Closer *(Close circle with a quote, poem, activity, question, etc.)*
One thing that I value, or appreciate, about my teacher is . . .

Circle Scripts

7. Green GTKY Circle #1 for Grades 6–12: Introducing Circle

Circle Opener *(You can use a quote, poem, activity, etc.)*
The Weather Report: Students will report how they are feeling as expressed by a type of weather.

Circle Guidelines *(Review norms of circle, explain talking piece and centerpiece)*
1. Respect the talking piece. You may pass it if you choose to.
2. What is said in circle stays in circle.
3. Safety (mandated reporting)
4. Speak from the heart!

Values Round *(A question or activity that will emphasize the values of those in circle)*
Think about someone who has been important to you. What values does that person exhibit that make him or her so important?

Discussion Round *(Questions that you can ask during circle)*
1. Conversation Cubes x 2
2. What was one highlight from your summer?
3. What has been one interesting thing about this school year up to this point?
4. Have you ever lived anywhere other than _____? If so, where have you lived?
5. Earlier in circle, we talked about someone who has been important to you. Is there someone in your life that you wish you spent more time with?
6. Tell us one thing that you are looking forward to.

Circle Closer *(Close circle with a quote, poem, activity, question, etc.)*
Two-Minute Connection: Students are given a slip of paper or an index card on which they write a question or topic that is on their minds. They then place the cards in a box (or some other type of container). These questions can be revisited whenever there is spare time.

8. Green GTKY Circle #2 for Grades 6–12

Circle Opener *(You can use a quote, poem, activity, etc.)*
I decided to stick with love. Hate is too great a burden.
—*Martin Luther King, Jr.*

Circle Guidelines *(Review norms of circle, explain talking piece and centerpiece)*
1. Respect the talking piece. You may pass it if you choose to.
2. What is said in circle stays in circle.
3. Safety (mandated reporting)
4. Speak from the heart!

Values Round *(A question or activity that will emphasize the values of those in circle)*
Think about someone who is important in your life. What is one value (or one way he or she treats you) that you admire?

Discussion Round *(Questions that you can ask during circle)*
1. Conversation Cubes x 2
2. If you could travel anywhere in the world, where would you go?
3. Who would you take with you if you could take only one person?
4. Have you always lived in this town? Stand up if you have lived somewhere different. Share with us where you have lived (using talking piece).
5. What is one thing that you struggle with in your life?
6. Do you respect your teachers? Why or why not? Do you think they respect you?
7. If you were to get a tattoo, what would it be?
8. Tell us one thing that you are excited about that is coming up in the near future.

Circle Closer *(Close circle with a quote, poem, activity, question, etc.)*
Tell us one new thing that you learned about someone while in circle today.

Circle Scripts

9. Green GTKY Circle #3 for Grades 6–12

Circle Opener *(You can use a quote, poem, activity, etc.)*
Listen, Linda! (video, https://www.youtube.com/watch?v=TP8RB7UZHKI). Before showing the video, tell the students this: The key to your success and my success is how well we listen to one another. I want to learn about you today in circle. I promise to listen. Please don't be like Mateo in this video!

Circle Guidelines *(Review norms of circle, explain talking piece and centerpiece)*
1. Respect the talking piece. You may pass it if you choose to.
2. What is said in circle stays in circle.
3. Safety (mandated reporting)
4. Speak from the heart!

Values Round *(A question or activity that will emphasize the values of those in circle)*
How does someone earn your respect?

Discussion Round *(Questions that you can ask during circle)*
1. Conversation Cubes
2. If you had one free period each day, and you could spend that time doing anything (appropriate) that you would like, what would you want to do?
3. If you could change one thing about this school, what would it be?
4. What is one thing that makes a teacher a great teacher? (Write these ideas down as the students share them. They will give you information about what they need.)
5. What is something that makes a student a great student?
6. What is something you wish was taught in school (specifically, in this class)?

Circle Closer *(Close circle with a quote, poem, activity, question, etc.)*
Compliment Toss: Have all the circle participants stand. Toss a soft ball to a participant and pay that person a compliment. Ask the participant to thank you for the compliment. Then you sit down. The student with the ball calls out another student's name, gives a compliment, tosses the ball to the student, and then sits down. This continues until only one student is standing. This special student can pick ANY student to receive the compliment.

Yellow CASEL Core Competencies Directory

Self-awareness (SAW)	1. Identifying emotions 2. Accurate self-perception 3. Recognizing strengths 4. Self-confidence 5. Self-efficacy
Self-management (SMG)	1. Impulse control 2. Stress management 3. Self-discipline 4. Self-motivation 5. Goal setting 6. Organizational skills
Social Awareness (SOA)	1. Perspective-taking 2. Empathy 3. Appreciating diversity 4. Respect for others
Relationship Skills (RSK)	1. Communication 2. Social engagement 3. Relationship building 4. Teamwork
Responsible Decision-making (RDM)	1. Identifying problems 2. Analyzing situations 3. Solving problems 4. Evaluating 5. Reflecting 6. Ethical responsibility

Source: https://casel.org/wp-content/uploads/2017/01/Competencies.pdf
Note: The above directory of core competencies applies to Yellow SEL (Social and Emotional Learning) Circles 10, 11, and 12, which follow.

Circle Scripts

10. Yellow SEL (Social and Emotional Learning) Circle #1: Anger

CASEL Core Competencies

Self-awareness	Self-management	Social Awareness	Relationship Skills	Responsible Decision-making
1, 2, 3, 4, 5	1, 2, 4	1, 2, 3, 4	1, 2, 3	1, 2, 3, 4, 5

Circle Opener *(You can use a quote, poem, activity, etc.)*
Read the poem "I Am Angry" or a similar poem about anger.

Circle Guidelines *(Review norms of circle, explain talking piece and centerpiece)*
1. Respect the talking piece. You may pass it if you choose to.
2. What is said in circle stays in circle.
3. Safety (mandated reporting)
4. Speak from the heart!

Values Round *(A question or activity that will emphasize the values of those in circle)*
Review values from the last relationship building circle.

Discussion Round *(Questions that you can ask during circle)*
1. Conversation Cubes or PowerPoint Circle Starters
2. *Get to Know Your "Out" Emotions: Anger* (video, https://www.youtube.com/watch?v=-HQIg3ZwAs0).
3. The trigger seen in the video was when the house of cards collapsed. What is something that can cause you to go from being calm to being angry?
4. How do you know when you are experiencing anger? What are some of your anger cues?
5. Share a story (possibly from when you were younger) about one time when you got so angry that you lost all control. This can be called "reaching the peak" of anger. (Try to find a video showing someone who may have reached the peak, if applicable.)
6. The goal is to use a strategy that will help us de-escalate while our anger cues are happening—and to do so before we hit our peak. What strategies do you use to de-escalate when your anger cues are happening? (Possibly create a list of these.)

Circle Closer *(Close circle with a quote, poem, activity, question, etc.)*
"Anger" is one letter short of "DANGER."

11. Yellow SEL Circle #2: Listening to Others

CASEL Core Competencies

Self-awareness	Self-management	Social Awareness	Relationship Skills	Responsible Decision-making
1, 3	1, 2	1, 2, 3, 4	1, 2, 3	1, 2, 4, 5

Circle Opener *(You can use a quote, poem, activity, etc.)*
Show a funny video about someone who is not actively listening.

Circle Guidelines *(Review norms of circle, explain talking piece and centerpiece)*
1. Respect the talking piece. You may pass it if you choose to.
2. What is said in circle stays in circle.
3. Safety (mandated reporting)
4. Speak from the heart!

Values Round *(A question or activity that will emphasize the values of those in circle)*
If you could give every person in the world one quality, what would it be and why?

Discussion Round *(Questions that you can ask during circle)*
1. Conversation Cubes
2. Who is someone in your home life that you wish would listen more closely to you?
3. When is it difficult for you to listen? What are some things that contribute to these difficulties?
4. What do good listeners do? (Create a list to post in the classroom.)
5. What is your favorite food? Favorite game? Favorite color?

Circle Closer *(Close circle with a quote, poem, activity, question, etc.)*
When you talk, you are only repeating what you already know. But if you listen, you may learn something new. —*Dalai Lama*

Circle Scripts

12. Yellow SEL Circle #3: Building Trust

CASEL Core Competencies

Self-awareness	Self-management	Social Awareness	Relationship Skills	Responsible Decision-making
1, 5	1, 3	1, 2, 3, 4	1, 2, 3, 4	1, 2, 4, 5, 6

Circle Opener *(You can use a quote, poem, activity, etc.)*
I used to trust a man's deeds after having listened to his words. Now having listened to a man's words I go on to observe his deeds. —*Confucius*

Circle Guidelines *(Review norms of circle, explain talking piece and centerpiece)*
1. Respect the talking piece. You may pass it if you choose to.
2. What is said in circle stays in circle.
3. Safety (mandated reporting)
4. Speak from the heart!

Values Round *(A question or activity that will emphasize the values of those in circle)*
What actions make someone a bad friend?

Discussion Round *(Questions that you can ask during circle)*
1. This week we have been studying Chinese philosophers. Look at the quote on the board and share what you think Confucius is saying about trust.
2. How important is trust to you? On a scale of 1–5, 1 being "not very important" and 5 being "very important," hold up the number of fingers that answers the question.
3. Who do you trust in your life and why?
4. Raise your hand if you . . .
    a. have ever had your trust broken
    b. have ever been hurt by someone who broke your trust
    c. have ever been untrustworthy yourself
5. Describe how trusting someone should feel. (Teacher-led question)
6. What qualities make someone trustworthy? How do you know you can trust someone?
7. Complete this sentence: Someone can trust me because . . .

Circle Closer *(Close circle with a quote, poem, activity, question, etc.)*
Simon Sinek on Building Trust through Committed Leadership (video, https://www.youtube.com/watch?v=lwuouSVtWAE). Adapted from an SEL circle created by Angela Panigrosso.

13. Yellow Curricular Circle #1: Arguments/Counter-arguments

Circle Opener *(You can use a quote, poem, activity, etc.)*
Review centerpiece (articles promoting or protesting hydraulic fracking).

Circle Guidelines *(Review norms of circle, explain talking piece and centerpiece)*
1. Respect the talking piece. You may pass it if you choose to.
2. What is said in circle stays in circle.
3. Safety (mandated reporting)
4. Speak from the heart!

Values Round *(A question or activity that will emphasize the values of those in circle)*
Respecting points of view review.

Discussion Round *(Questions that you can ask during circle)*
1. If you received $100,000 without needing to do anything for it, what would you do with the money?
2. (Show Canada energy video.) Why would an energy company want to highlight the positives of natural gas? (In the discussion, move away from gasoline and petroleum-based products to natural gas and cleaner energy.)
3. (Show fracking information video.) Representatives from Chesapeake Gas Company show up at your front door, just 10 minutes down the road in Pennsylvania. You have 20 acres of land. They offer you $100,000 a year to be able to drill for natural gas on your land. Would you let them? Why? Write down your reason.
4. Now we are going to change the situation. You live right across the border in New York. By law, you are not allowed to lease your land to the gas company. However, the water source you use is the same source that is used in Pennsylvania. (Show sink video.) Did your opinion change? If so, this is a counter-argument to what you said earlier.

Circle Scripts

5. What would you do if you were the governor of New York? Would you choose yes or no to fracking? Write down two reasons.

Circle Closer *(Close circle with a quote, poem, activity, question, etc.)*
The toughest questions often do not have the easiest answers. To find our own answers to difficult questions, we need to investigate the arguments and counter-arguments put forth by people with different opinions.

14. Yellow Curricular Circle #2: Jim Crow/Segregation Laws

Circle Opener *(You can use a quote, poem, activity, etc.)*
Choose sections of Langston Hughes's poem "Let America Be Great Again" to read to the class.

Circle Guidelines *(Review norms of circle, explain talking piece and centerpiece)*
1. Respect the talking piece. You may pass it if you choose to.
2. What is said in circle stays in circle.
3. Safety (mandated reporting)
4. Speak from the heart!

Values Round *(A question or activity that will emphasize the values of those in circle)*
How comfortable are you talking about race? Hold up the number of fingers that show how you are feeling. (Fist-to-Five—one finger is something along the lines of terrible, all five fingers is fantastic.)

Discussion Round *(Questions that you can ask during circle)*
1. What do you need from the group today so you can feel that you can share openly and honestly?
2. How does this picture make you feel (show a photo of an experience from the current era)? What thoughts come to mind?
3. Why would people support the idea of segregation?
4. Do you feel times have changed for the better or for the worse since the Civil Rights Act was passed?
5. If you could send a message from modern times back to the times of segregation, what would it be?
6. What are some ways that we can fight segregation today?

Circle Closer *(Close circle with a quote, poem, activity, question, etc.)*

It is not possible to be in favor of justice for some people and not be in favor of justice for all people. —*Martin Luther King, Jr.*

15. Yellow Curricular Circle #3: Positive and Negative Thinking

Circle Opener *(You can use a quote, poem, activity, etc.)*
Ball of Clay: The student who starts the activity pretends to have a ball of clay and shapes it into an object, then mimes an action with the imaginary object that shows what it is used for. The rest of the participants give a silent thumbs-up when they think they have figured out what the object is. The student then rolls the imaginary object back into a ball of clay and passes it to the next person. Repeat the process until everyone has had a turn. This simple game allows people to express their creativity and personality nonverbally, and begins circle on a note of fun. Note: This activity does not use a talking piece. We say that the ball of clay is the talking piece.

Circle Guidelines *(Review norms of circle, explain talking piece and centerpiece)*
1. Respect the talking piece. You may pass it if you choose to.
2. What is said in circle stays in circle
3. Safety (mandated reporting)
4. Speak from the heart!

Values Round
None

Discussion Round *(Questions that you can ask during circle)*
1. What is one skill or talent that you wish you had?
2. Name one thing about yourself that you would like to grow or improve in.
3. The number line on the board shows two words that you can talk about in math class (especially when talking about graphs, temperature, or money). The word "positive" in math means "above zero" and is often symbolized by the color green. Positive thinking means that you focus on your strengths instead of your weaknesses. "I CAN" statements are an example. Share with us a positive thought that you have about yourself.
4. The word "negative" in math means "below zero." It is often symbolized by the color red. Negative thinking means that you focus on weaknesses instead of good qualities or hope. "I CAN'T" statements are an example. Share with us an "I CAN'T" example that you've used or that you've heard

Circle Scripts

someone else use. Think about this situation: You are in class and you need a pencil. You call to a friend of yours across the room and ask to borrow his pencil. The teacher gets angry and says to you in front of the class, "You are being a distraction to this class. I can't do my job when you do that. You need to move your seat to the corner of the room." Those of you who are still sitting in circle, look behind your chair and take the sticky note off it. The sticky note will be either red or green. If you have a red sticky note, I'd like you to write down a negative thought that you could have for the situation. If you have a green sticky note, I'd like you to write down a positive thought you could have for the situation. Now we are going to place your sticky notes on the number line by how positive or negative you think the thoughts are.
5. What did you mention earlier as the one thing that you would like to improve in? What positive thought could help you improve?

Circle Closer *(Close circle with a quote, poem, activity, question, etc.)*
Keep your thoughts positive because your thoughts become your words.
Keep your words positive because your words become your behavior.
Keep your behavior positive because your behavior becomes your habits.
Keep your habits positive because your habits become your values.
Keep your values positive because your values become your destiny.
—*Gandhi*

16. Red Reactive Circle #1: Classroom Issues

Circle Opener *(You can use a quote, poem, activity, etc.)*
The way you treat people says a lot about who you are. Be careful. Your actions are screaming over your words.

Circle Guidelines *(Review norms of circle, explain talking piece and centerpiece)*
1. Respect the talking piece. You may pass it if you choose to.
2. What is said in circle stays in circle.
3. Safety (mandated reporting)
4. Speak from the heart!
5. We will not use specific names during circle today.

Values Round *(A question or activity that will emphasize the values of those in circle)*

What do you need from each person in circle so you feel you can share openly and honestly?

Discussion Round *(Questions that you can ask during circle)*
1. What made the best teacher you ever had such a great teacher?
2. To teacher: How do you feel each day after leaving this class? (Write the teacher's response on chart paper.) Ask students for a thumbs-up or a thumbs-down if this is their intention on a daily basis.
3. To students: How do you feel each day after leaving this class? (Write the students' responses on chart paper.) Did you know that you were making people feel like this on a daily basis?
4. What is one thing that interferes with your learning or peace of mind while you are in this classroom?
5. What is something you can do to help create a better culture and atmosphere in this classroom?
6. Share with us something you are looking forward to doing in the near future.

Circle Closer *(Close circle with a quote, poem, activity, question, etc.)*
Find someone to exchange a handshake, fist bump, or high five with before we leave. Let that person know that you are looking forward to a fresh start when we meet again.

17. Red Reactive Circle #2: Struggling Classes

Circle Opener *(You can use a quote, poem, activity, etc.)*
Maturity is not measured by age. It's an attitude built by experience.
—*Unknown*

Circle Guidelines *(Review norms of circle, explain talking piece and centerpiece)*
1. Respect the talking piece. You may pass it if you choose to.
2. What is said in circle stays in circle.
3. Safety (mandated reporting)
4. Speak from the heart!
5. We will not use specific names in circle today.

Values Round *(A question or activity that will emphasize the values of those in circle)*
How do you want others to treat you?

Circle Scripts

Discussion Round *(Questions that you can ask during circle)*
1. Conversation Cubes x 2
2. What types of behaviors are occurring in this classroom that are interfering with everyone's ability to learn? (Use index cards if need be or write ideas on chart paper or board. (Vote for two. Pick top one or two issues to focus on.)
3. When these (one or two) things happen, how does it make you feel? OR how does it affect you personally?
4. Let's be honest: How many of you, with a show of hands, contribute to this behavior on a weekly basis or even occasionally?
5. (Read to group:) To those who exhibit these behaviors, did you have any idea that you were possibly making others feel (share ideas from previous question).
6. Needs question: What can you do or offer that will make this group work the best it can?
7. When other students are acting out with these behaviors that make it difficult for you to be successful in the classroom, do you feel comfortable enough to let them know how their actions are affecting you? (Thumbs-up or thumbs-down.) It seems that we've created a classroom culture in which we do not feel able to talk about how some people's actions are affecting the way we feel.
8. Clean Slate: I'd like each of you to let the class know if it is okay for them to tell you when you are making it difficult for them to learn or do their job. This is also a time when you can apologize for past behavior if you choose to.

Circle Closer *(Close circle with a quote, poem, activity, question, etc.)*
Recognize that every interaction you have is an opportunity to make a positive impact on others. —Shep Hyken

18. Green GTKY Staff Circle #1: Relationship Building

Circle Opener *(You can use a quote, poem, activity, etc.)*
At their core, organizations are just giant networks of relationships. So if you fail to build those relationships, your chances of succeeding are not very high.

CIRCLE SCRIPTS

Circle Guidelines *(Review norms of circle, explain talking piece and centerpiece)*
1. Respect the talking piece. You may pass it if you choose to.
2. What is said in circle stays in circle.
3. Speak from the heart!

Values Round *(A question or activity that will emphasize the values of those in circle)*
What do you need from our group so that you feel you can share openly and honestly in circle today?

Who was your favorite teacher in your K–12 years? What is one thing that made that teacher stand above the others that you had?

Discussion Round *(Questions that you can ask during circle)*
1. Share with us your name, where you went to high school, and how long you have been teaching.
2. Conversation Cubes
3. If you could have a faucet that dispensed any drink that you would like, what would you want to come from it?
4. What is one thing you would like to see change with regard to your experience as a teacher/educator?
5. Share with us something about yourself that most people here would not know.
6. Share with us one thing that you are looking forward to in the near future.
7. Extra-time question: If you could travel anywhere in the world right now, where would you go AND if you could take only one living person with you, who would it be?

Circle Closer *(Close circle with a quote, poem, activity, question, etc.)*
Three things should happen in a quality relationship building circle. First, the participants should learn something new about one another. Second, the participants should learn something new about the facilitator. Finally, the facilitator should learn something new about the participants. If those three things happen, we should consider circle a success. Follow up with a Fist-to-Five on their experience in an adult circle.

19. Green GTKY Staff Circle #2: Beginning the Year

Circle Opener *(You can use a quote, poem, activity, etc.)*
Every Kid Needs a Champion (The Power of Relationships), by Rita Pierson. Whole-group video. https://www.youtube.com/watch?v=SFnMTHhKdkw&t=15s.

Circle Guidelines *(Review norms of circle, explain talking piece and centerpiece.)*
1. Respect the talking piece. You may pass it if you choose to.
2. What is said in circle stays in circle.
3. Speak from the heart!

Values Round *(A question or activity that will emphasize the values of those in circle)*
What do you need from our group so that you feel that you can share openly and honestly in circle today?

Tell us about someone who has been a great influence on you. What strength or character trait did that person instill in you that you benefited from today?

Discussion Round *(Questions that you can ask during circle)*
1. Share with us your name, position, and one fun fact about the past summer.
2. What went through your mind last night (or the night before your first day back)?
3. Share with us one positive moment (or learning experience) that you had last year (in the classroom, on the job, in college, etc.).
4. Share with us one way you create (or plan to create) community and culture within your classroom.
5. Think of a time when going out of your way to create (or build upon) a relationship led to a fantastic outcome.
6. Extra-time question: If you could teach a different grade level and/or subject, what would you teach and why?

Circle Closer *(Close circle with a quote, poem, activity, question, etc.)*
We can do this! We are educators. We were born to make a difference!

—*Rita Pierson*

20. Green GTKY Staff Circle #3: Exploring School/Staff Issues

Circle Opener *(You can use a quote, poem, activity, etc.)*
The Weather Report: The facilitator takes the pulse of how participants are feeling by using a weather analogy. For example, a participant might share that at the close of circle, his weather report is sunny, while another might indicate that hers is overcast with a chance of rain. Of course, there is no "correct" response. The purpose is for participants to have the opportunity to honestly express how they are feeling and for the facilitator to use that information to assess the emotional status of the members of the circle.

Circle Guidelines *(Review norms of circle, explain talking piece and centerpiece)*
1. This is the talking piece. You may pass it if you choose to.
2. What is said in circle stays in circle.
3. Speak from the heart!

Values Round *(A question or activity that will emphasize the values of those in circle)*
What do you need from our group so that you feel you can share openly and honestly in circle today? (This question can be omitted if it was asked in a previous circle and this circle includes the same participants.)

Discussion Round *(Questions that you can ask during circle)*
1. Share with us an embarrassing moment (or just a moment of learning) that you can laugh at now. (Builds understanding of one another and can create empathy.)
2. What has been the single hardest part of this school year for you? (Helps us explore issues or concerns.)
3. What can we do as individuals to create a healthy workplace for all of us? (Taking responsibility.)
4. Explain in one sentence how you would be able to tell if things are getting better. (Clarifying expectations about the future.)
5. Share with us something that you are looking forward to doing outside of school. (Building community.)

Circle Closer *(Close circle with a quote, poem, activity, question, etc.)*
When we have inner peace, we can be at peace with those around us. When our community is in a state of peace, it can share that peace with neighboring communities [our students]. —*Dalai Lama*

PART III

Circle Building Tools

Part III provides tools that can be used for building circles. Circle Openers and Circle Closers appear together in this list. Remember, you can always use quotes to open or close circle. The Internet is your friend when it comes to finding unique quotes!

Openers and Closers

1. **My Favorite:** Students answer a question about their favorite something. If this is an introductory circle, have them state their names.
2. **Suffix-Speak:** Students tell one thing that they enjoy doing that ends in the suffix *–ing*.
3. **Compliment Toss:** Have all the circle participants stand. Toss a soft ball to one of them and pay that person a compliment. Ask him or her to thank you for the compliment. Then you sit down. The student with the ball calls out another student's name, gives a compliment, tosses the ball to the student, and then sits down. This continues until only one student is standing. This special student can pick ANY other student to receive a compliment.
4. **On Your Feet!** Have one of the students in the circle use the talking piece to ask a question. Participants stand up if they can answer "yes" to the question. Pass the talking piece around the circle to allow everyone an opportunity to speak.
5. **It Gets Worse:** Have students come up with one thing that can make a situation worse when they get angry.
6. **Temperature:** Have students write a temperature on an index card. Place all the cards on a large thermometer (drawn on the board or, ideally, made in the middle of the circle). The temperature represents how they are feeling: the lower the temperature, the worse they feel, and the higher the temperature, the better they feel. If students need a reference point, the facilitator could designate a temperature that means they are feeling average.
7. **It's All Mime!** Students mime certain feelings based on situations described by the facilitator. Examples: How would you look if you slammed your finger in a door? If you lost your bike? If your friend found your bike? If your favorite song came on the radio? If you had to try a food that you didn't like? If you heard a really loud sound? If you scraped your knee on the blacktop?
8. **Memory Menu:** One by one, participants share what their favorite foods are. The first person says his favorite food. The second person says the first person's favorite food and her own. The third person says the first and second persons' favorite foods and then adds his own. This

CIRCLE BUILDING TOOLS

continues as the talking piece goes around the circle. Have students use a silent cue to ask for help if they forget.

9. **Quiet Circle-Up!** Students quietly stand up and, without speaking, arrange themselves in some particular order. Examples include alphabetical order of names, birth month, birthday, number of pets, etc.
10. **Follow the Leader:** The facilitator walks up to one person in the circle and starts a motion (like snapping fingers, patting thighs, etc.). Then he or she moves around the circle until everyone is copying this motion. Start a new motion once the circle has been completed.
11. **My Weekend:** Students state their names and one activity that they like to do on the weekend.
12. **That's Not Fair:** Participants finish this sentence: It's not fair when _____.
13. **Count to 10:** Students work together as a group to count to 10. There is one twist: Only one person can say one number at a time. If more than one person says the next number, the counting must start over at 1. The facilitator keeps track of how many attempts it takes.
14. **"21":** Students can say up to three numbers at a time. Count in order until someone has to say "21." That person is eliminated from the game. The class in unison says "Good morning" or "Good afternoon" to the student who has been eliminated. Restart each round at 1 and play until only one person remains.
15. **Where the Wind Blows:** One person starts the game by standing in the middle of the circle and telling the group something he or she has never done before. For example, "I've never been on a train," "I've never been to a dance," "I've never been to Florida," "I've never had a cat." If the statement also applies to someone else sitting in the circle, that person has to move from his or her seat to a different seat. The person in the middle will need to try to sit down. One person will remain standing. The standing person starts a new round by making a different statement. People cannot move to seats on their immediate left or right, but they can sit two seats away from their current places.
16. **Object Story:** Collect a number of everyday objects and place them in a canvas bag, a basket, or a box. Some suggestions are pencil or pen, key ring, mobile phone, small toy, stuffed animal. Also include some unusual items, such as a wig, a feather, a silly photograph, or a rock. Pass the container around, inviting each student to reach in and choose an item without looking. The leader begins a story with a sentence that includes the name of the object he or she is holding. After 10 seconds (or longer if you wish) the next student continues the story, mentioning the object he has chosen. Continue until every student has added to the

Circle Building Tools

story. Another fun storytelling icebreaker begins with the leader starting a story. After a sentence or two setting the scene, the leader ends his or her part of the story with "Suddenly . . . " and trails off. The student whose turn it is next completes the "Suddenly" statement that the leader began, contributes whatever else he or she wishes to add, and ends with beginning his or her own new "Suddenly . . . " sentence. Each student ends his contribution to the growing story the same way, with "Suddenly. . . . " It's fun to record the story and play it back after all the students have added their sentences. This storytelling icebreaker is quick, easy, and can be used with any size group.

17. **Word Link:** For this word association game, the first person in the circle says any word he or she wishes. The second person links another word to the first. This continues around the circle, with each person adding another word. For example, the first person might say, "Green." The second person adds, "Lettuce." The third person adds, "Salad." Therefore, by person number three, you have "Green lettuce salad." Allow only five seconds for each word link and eliminate those who cannot think of a word or who take too long to do so. The last two students are the winners.

18. **Ball of Clay:** The student who starts the activity pretends to have a ball of clay and shapes it into an object, then mimes an action with the imaginary object that shows what it is used for. The rest of the participants give a silent thumbs-up when they think they have figured out what the object is. The student then rolls the imaginary object back into a ball of clay and passes it to the next person. Repeat the process until everyone has had a turn. This simple game allows everyone to express creativity and personality nonverbally and begins circle with a bit of fun. Note: This activity does not use a talking piece. We say that the ball of clay is the talking piece.

19. **The Quietest Sound:** Tell students that the whole group is going to see how long they can hear the sound of a bell. Have them raise their hands and close their eyes. After they first hear the bell, they should slowly lower their hands as the sound of the bell fades, finally bringing their hands to rest in their laps when they can no longer hear it.

20. **Outer and Inner Voice:** This is an extension of the previous activity. We are listening to the true voice of the bell. Ask the students to notice if, when they can no longer hear the bell with their ears, its tone continues to resonate within them. As with the previous activity, they will lower their arms and rest their hands when they can no longer hear the bell, but then allow their hands to rise slightly if there is some way in which the bell is still resonating for them.

CIRCLE BUILDING TOOLS

21. **Secret Voice:** This is an extension of the previous two activities. Explain that the bell can speak only in its one true voice, but that humans can choose a variety of voices. Suggest that when the voice of the bell is resonating, some thought or image will appear in the imagination. This is the "secret voice" that we hear when we listen to ourselves. Have the students lift their hands when their imagination presents something in response to the tone of the bell. Use the talking piece to share in the circle.

22. **Speaking with One Voice:** This activity helps align vocal energy. Choose a syllable such as "ah" or "oh." Have students rest their hands in their laps. Together, say the syllable very quietly. Lead the class by raising your hands and increasing the volume until everyone's hands are straight up and the volume is at maximum level. After a pause, suddenly drop your hands and be silent. Repeat until the group can hold the silence for five seconds after everyone's hands have dropped. If you wish, you can ask a student who breaks the silence early to be "it" and lead the next round.

23. **Snap:** Give each of the students a card. They have to find their partner, who will be the one with the matching card. Then repeat the same exercise, but this time they have to do it without talking. Use picture cards or playing cards.

24. **All Aboard:** Divide the class into five to ten groups. Give each group several paper spots. Can they all stand on the spots? Now take away one spot, two spots, three spots, etc., and have the students hold still for three seconds without touching the floor itself. You can also use hoops for this, or challenge the whole class to stand inside a hoop.

25. **All Change:** The students stand in a circle, and the teacher taps one on the shoulder. That person starts an action (e.g., clapping), which the others have to follow. The teacher taps another student on the shoulder, and the group changes to a new action selected by that person.

26. **Handwriting:** Working in pairs, the students take turns drawing a shape on their partner's hand using a finger. While one of them is drawing, the partner must close his or her eyes and guess what the shape is. In a circle, the students are to pass the shape around without talking and see if the shape is the same at the end.

27. **Whose Voice Is That?** Students stand in a circle. One in the middle is blindfolded. Somebody from the circle makes an animal noise, and the blindfolded person has to guess who made the sound.

28. **Jigsaws:** Give every participant part of a jigsaw puzzle. He or she has to find which other people have the rest of the puzzle and then put it together. Aim to work cooperatively to complete the puzzle as quickly as possible. You'll need a selection of laminated pictures or puzzle pieces.

Circle Building Tools

29. **Through the Hoop:** Have the students stand in a big circle. Can everyone climb through the hoop? Repeat the task with everyone holding hands. Repeat the task, but don't allow the students to use their hands. Can they repeat the task with only one person touching the hoop? You can also set this game up so smaller groups are racing one another to get the hoop around the circle first.
30. **Feely Bag:** Have the students feel themed objects in a bag and guess what they are.
31. **Jingle Ball Pass:** Participants must pass the jingle ball around the circle without making a sound. Then have them pass it under and over their heads, side to side, etc.
32. **Sort the Cards:** Give everybody one card. The participants have to sort themselves into each suit: clubs, spades, hearts, and diamonds. To make it more complicated, they then have to put themselves in the order A, 1, 2, 3, 4, 5, 6, 7, 8, 9, 10, J, Q, K.
33. **My Rules!** One student leaves the classroom. While he or she is gone, the rest of the group think up a new rule, e.g., cross your legs when answering a question or use words starting with the first letter of your name. The student rejoins the group and has to guess the secret rule by asking questions and watching what the other students do. (This can be done in smaller groups, too.)
34. **Balloon Keepie-Uppie:** Have the participants sit on the floor in groups of four to eight. The goal is to keep a balloon or balloons in the air. Try it using various body parts, with no hands, with just the head, etc.
35. **Who Am I?** Give everyone in the group a forehead sticker that has the name of a famous character written on it, e.g., Spider-Man. The students have to guess who they are and can answer only yes or no to one another's questions.
36. **Circle Filled with Statues:** Use the talking piece for this activity. You will want a bell or something else that can make an audible sound. Begin by modeling the activity. Once the bell chimes, everyone in the classroom will try to re-create, or copy, the statue pose of the person who has the talking piece. Each student should be allowed 8 to 10 seconds before the talking piece is passed and a new statue is posed. Let the talking piece travel around the entire circle.
37. **What's on the Tray?** Place up to 10 things on a tray (or on a projection screen). Give the students one or two minutes to memorize as many of the items as they can. When time is up, remove the tray (or take down the images), pass the talking piece around, and ask the students to write down as many things as they can remember. For an extended circle, you could increase the number of items to 20. Create questions to follow that

would discuss interesting ways to help us remember such things.
38. **What Would You Do If You Were Me?** The teacher shares an everyday problem or a specific dilemma that he or she is facing or has faced. Once the situation is framed, the participants have 30 seconds of think time and then the teacher asks them what they would have done if they had had that problem.
39. **Deep Breathing:** Use a chime or bell for this activity. Have participants breathe in deeply through their noses. Ring the bell and have students hold their breath until the sound of the bell or chime fades away. Then have students breathe quietly out of their mouths. Repeat three to five times.
40. **Centerpiece Review:** Start with an empty centerpiece (or just your mat/flag/cloth—whatever you use). Ask students to recall what was in the centerpiece from the last meeting. Retell some of the stories about the pieces as the students remember them.

Values Round Questions

1. Think of someone in your life who is very important to you. What value or strength has that person instilled in you?
2. What do you need from the others in circle so that you feel you can share openly and honestly?
3. Share with us one way that you would like others to see you.
4. How do you want others to treat you?
5. If you had to give every person one quality, what would it be and why?
6. What is the most important quality for a leader to have?
7. How do you choose your friends?
8. Who is one person that you wish you had more time for in your life?
9. Who is the most important person in your life and what could you do to enhance your relationship with that person?
10. What is the most important thing that makes a relationship successful?
11. What could we do to protect and promote the unity of our group?
12. What is one thing you hope will happen with this group?
13. What are three qualities you want your friends to have?
14. What makes a good friend?
15. What are three qualities you admire in one of your parents?
16. What is one thing that you hope people will say about you after you die?
17. If you could give every human being one quality, what would it be and why?
18. What is the meanest thing someone could say to you?
19. What is something you like about yourself?

Circle Building Tools

20. What hurts your feelings?
21. What's the best compliment you've ever gotten?
22. What makes someone a bad friend?
23. What are the qualities you would look for in someone you want to date?
24. Do you believe in God? Why or why not?
25. What do you think is the meaning of life?
26. How do people earn respect?
27. How would you change the world if you could?
28. Do you think it's ever okay to lie? If so, in what kinds of situations?
29. What are three things that you are grateful for today?
30. What is an important change you want to see in yourself?
31. What do you think the key to happiness is?
32. Does it matter if a person makes a moral or immoral choice, if no one ever knows?
33. If someone you loved was very sick but could not afford the medicine to get better, would it be okay to steal the medicine?
34. Do adults automatically deserve respect? How do you earn respect?
35. What do you think makes the most difference in how kids do at school? Hard work, innate ability, parental supervision, peer attitudes, how good the school is?
36. What are the different kinds of courage? How do you define bravery?
37. What do you think leadership is? What makes a good leader?
38. Who is an important person from your life who has taught you valuable things?
39. Who is a teacher you have had that you admire or appreciate?
40. What do your friends want from you the most?
41. What does your family want from you the most?
42. When did you last do something for nothing in return?
43. What's your greatest achievement to date?
44. How would you hate to be described?
45. Is trust more important than love, or is it the other way around?
46. If you woke up tomorrow with a habit gone, what would it be?
47. What risk do you need to take?
48. Do you need to see things before you believe them?
49. What is something that grabs your heart?
50. What is something that gives you hope?
51. Who is someone that did something nice for you? Tell us about the person and what he or she did.

Discussion Round Questions

1. About Me

Do you have any recurring dreams? If so, describe them.
What is the meanest thing someone could say to you?
Who would play you if your life were a movie?
What is something that you would like to invent?
What is your favorite song?
Do you believe in heaven? What does yours look like? Is it different for everyone?
What do you first notice when you meet a person?
What is the most beautiful thing you have ever seen?
What would the cover of a book about you look like?
Who is a person you would like to trade places with?
What do you say when you talk to yourself?
What is one of the most adventurous things you've ever done?
What is the farthest you've been from home? Where was it?
What is something that you like about yourself?
What is one of your favorite books?
What was the last book that you read?
Who is your best friend?
Who was your best friend when you were younger?
What is one of your first memories?
Is there someone that you would like to repair a relationship with?
What is your favorite possession?
Do you have a nickname (and what is the story behind it)?
When do you get discouraged?
When do you feel the most vulnerable?
What's your favorite musical group?
What is your favorite outfit to wear?
What is one regret you have from _____ (this week, last year)?
What is your least favorite chore to do?
Who do you wish would pay more attention to you?
What's the most difficult thing for you to do?
Do you have a visible scar? If so, how did you get it?
What one possession do you value the most?
What is your least favorite sound in the world?
Have you lived anywhere other than this city/town? If so, where?
What is something that teachers or parents repeat over and over again?
What would you order as your final meal?

Circle Building Tools

How would you spend $100?
How would you spend $1,000?
What would your theme song be if you could have one playing each day as you walked into school?
What is your favorite animal?
Where were you born? What hospital?
What is your favorite flower?
What was/is your favorite toy from childhood?
Who is your favorite cartoon or movie character?
What is your favorite activity with friends?
What is one opportunity you have had in the last week/month/year to help someone?
What is the best thing that has happened to you recently?
What is your favorite ice cream flavor and your favorite topping to put on ice cream?
What is one thing that has made you laugh this week?
Who would you take on vacation with you if you could take only one person?
What is your favorite kind of fruit?
What's the biggest struggle you are facing right now?
What is the scariest thing you've ever done?
What one thing would you change about your house or room if you could?
What is one personal tragedy you have overcome?
What was the last movie you saw in a theater?
What's one of your best memories?
What do you worry about the most?
What helps you feel better when you're sad or worried?
What can I do to help you when you're sad or worried?
How often do you feel sad?
When was the last time that you felt angry?
What does your perfect day look like?
Who would you like to listen more closely to you?
Do you have any friends you're concerned about right now?
Are you happy with the number of friends you have?
Do you ever feel lonely or left out?
Has anyone ever been a bad friend to you?
What do you think real popularity looks like?
Would you consider yourself more shy or more outgoing?
Is there anyone at school that you would like to get to know better?
What's your most embarrassing moment?
What makes a healthy relationship?
Do you know anyone who's gay? Does anyone treat that person differently?

What do you think about that?
How old do you think you have to be to fall in love? What about get married?
What is something you wish I would do more of?
What is something you wish I would do less of?
How do you picture God?
Who do you think looks up to you?
What is your favorite word?
What is your least favorite word?
What is your favorite TV show?
What is your favorite video game?
What is your favorite website?
Why do you think kids put rings in their eyebrows and noses and belly buttons?
Why do you think people get tattoos?
Would you rather live in a castle, on a spaceship, or underground?
Who is or was your favorite teacher? Why?
What is the difference between being smart and being wise?
What do you know how to do that you could teach someone else?
How do you feel when someone is angry with you? How do you act?
Why do you think it's illegal for kids under the age of 21 to drink alcohol?
Why are marijuana and other drugs illegal?
What would you do if you were in a car and the driver had been drinking or doing drugs?
Have you been to a party like that? Have you ever been offered a drink? A marijuana cigarette or other drugs?
What movie could you watch over and over?
What is your favorite dessert?
What's your favorite style of music?
What's your least favorite type of candy?
What is something you do that bothers people around you?
What are two things that you do every day?
What is your favorite fictional story?
What do you like to do on rainy days?
What is something that you have just done for the first time?
What is something that you are thankful for?
What is something that is going on in the world/news that you are really worried about?
What is your favorite season?
What was your biggest worry five years ago? Do you still feel the same about it at this moment?

Circle Building Tools

What advice would you give yourself if you could go back to the time when you were five?
What promises have you not fulfilled for yourself?
What is one law that you would like to change?
What is the most beautiful thing that you have ever seen?
Who do you wish you had met sooner in life?
What was the last thing that you had to talk yourself out of?
How do you feel on (any day of the week)?
What would you ask your hero if you had the opportunity to speak to him or her?
What's your greatest achievement to date?
What is something that you wish you knew and you are embarrassed that you don't know?
Do you set goals or just let life happen?
What is a mistake that you have made that you are okay with?
What is one event that you would like to erase from your past?
What is something that makes you unique?
What bad experience keeps happening to you over and over again?
What is something that you have stopped doing but used to love and do all the time?
When did you last regret something you said?
What was something you had to do this week that you did not enjoy?
Did you visit anyone this week? If so, who?
How is your bedroom decorated?
Do you have a bike? What does it look like?
Who is someone you know who always makes you smile or laugh?
What was a time when you were in an uncomfortable situation?
What was a time when you felt you did the right thing even though it may not have been "cool"?
What was a time when you resolved a conflict (argument, fight, etc.) in a way that made everyone feel good?
Have you ever done something that was really difficult but that ended up teaching you a valuable lesson? What was it?
What is something that you have forgiven someone for? (No names)
The color _____ reminds you of _____.

2. The Future

What is one thing that you would like to learn about your future?
What do you want to do after you graduate from high school?
What electronic device would you like to own?
What would you like to be doing in five years?

What would you like to be doing in ten years?
What is your goal in life?
What are you dreaming about for your life?
What would you like to have the biggest collection of?
What part of your future are you most excited about?
What is something that you would like to try for the first time?
When you are surprised with one free hour during the day, how do you spend it?
What disease would you like to cure?
What is your dream car?
What thing doesn't exist that someone needs to invent?
What would the perfect birthday party look like?
What do you think happens after a person dies?
When you're on your deathbed, what would you want to look back and remember?
Where would you go if you had a time machine and could travel anywhere in any time?
How would you use an extra room in your house if you had one?
Where (what city or location) would you like to live when you get older?
Where do you want to go to college?
What is something that you really want to do in your lifetime?
What is the first thing you would do if you became president?
What is something that you have not done but would like to try?
What's your top priority in life?
Who is someone that you would like to talk to that you haven't talked to in a while?
Is there anything about your future that scares you? If so, what is it?
If you had to move tomorrow, where would you go?
What would you dare yourself to do in a game of Truth or Dare?
What would you do with the rest of your life if money was not an issue?

3. School

If you could change one thing about your school, what would it be?
If we could have circle anywhere, where would you like to have it?
What was the best (or worst) thing that happened at school today?
What was your favorite part of lunch or recess?
What part of the day do you look forward to?
What part of the day do you not look forward to?
Which class are you learning the most in?
Which class are you learning the least in?
Are there any bullies at your school? (No names)

Circle Building Tools

Have you ever been targeted by a bully?
How do you deal with a bully?
What does it mean to be popular at your school?
Do you respect your teachers? Why or why not? Do you think they respect you?
Do you think it makes sense to admit students to a college on the basis of academic achievement only or should an attempt be made to take into account racial and ethnic diversity of the student body as well? Explain.
Do you think kids from wealthier schools have an unfair advantage? Why or why not?
How do you feel when someone is angry with you? How do you act?
Why do you think it's illegal for kids under the age of 21 to drink alcohol?
Why are marijuana and other drugs illegal?
What would you do if you were in a car and the driver had been drinking or doing drugs?
Have you been to a party like that? Have you ever been offered a drink? A marijuana cigarette or other drugs?
Do you think peer pressure is a real thing?
Have you ever felt peer pressure?
Do some people struggle with peer pressure more than others?
Does teasing often go too far in your experience?
Do all kids who get teased believe it is bullying?
Do the kids who aren't leading the teasing feel they have to join in?
Describe some ways in which kids who are teased react to the teasing.
Do people who are being teased stick up for themselves?
Does sticking up for yourself when being bullied or teased usually work out?
What do you think the teasing does to the person being teased?
Are you proud to be a student at your school? Why or why not?
Do you like the grade you are in more or less than the one you were in last year?

4. The Community

What is the biggest problem in your community?
Where is your favorite place to eat?
What would you show a person who is new to your area?
What place do you most enjoy visiting in your community?
What would you change about your community?
Do you have pride in your community? Why or why not?

CIRCLE BUILDING TOOLS

5. My Family

What is your favorite part about being in your family?
What's one thing you like about your mom/dad?
How would you describe your grandparents?
How often do/did you get to see your grandparents?
Did you get to know any of your great-grandparents? If so, how old were you when they passed away?
How many children would you like to have?
How many siblings do you have?
What are your relationships with your siblings like?
What do you like most about your parents?
Is there anything you wish your family would do together more often?
Do you think the discipline in your family is fair? What would you change?
What is the thing you like best about your family?
What are the names of your siblings or children?
How do you like being a big/little sister/brother?
Where does your dad/mom work?
What is your favorite thing to do as a family?
Do you have any pets? If so, what kind?
What are the names of your pets?
Does your family go on a vacation each year?
Tell us about a time when you disagreed with your parents/guardians but now realize that they were right.

6. If You Could . . .

If you could be a famous athlete, actor, writer, or musician, who would you choose and why?
If you were invisible, where would you go?
If you could snap your fingers twice and appear anywhere in the world, where would you go?
If you could stay one age forever, what would it be?
If you could invent a holiday, what and when would it be?
If you died today, what would you wish you had done?
If you had one more day to live, how would you spend it?
If you could choose one superpower, what would it be?
If you could travel back in time, which event would you like to witness?
If you could have an unlimited gift card to any one restaurant, which would you choose?
If you could have a bottomless drink dispenser in your kitchen—like a faucet

Circle Building Tools

- that dispensed any one drink anytime you wanted it—which drink would you choose?
- If you had $10 to spend, how would you spend it?
- If one of your five senses could have supernatural abilities, which sense would you choose?
- If you could have any animal in the world as a pet, what animal would you choose?
- If you could choose any method of transportation to travel, what would you choose?
- If you could travel anywhere in the world, where would you go?
- If you could design your own TV channel, what would be the theme?
- If you could achieve the highest level of education in any one subject, which would you choose?
- If you could be famous, would you?
- If you were to get a tattoo, what would it be?
- If you could have any job in the world, what would it be?
- If you could have a conversation with anyone in history, who would it be? What would you want to ask that person?
- If you could change one thing about your appearance, what would it be?
- If you could change your gender, would you? Why or why not?
- If you could improve any talent, what would it be?
- If someone could tell you your future, would you let them?
- What would you change if you could change one thing from history?
- If you could have dinner with anyone, living or dead, who would it be and why?
- If you had to wear a shirt with any one word on it for a month, what would it say?
- If you could give advice to a celebrity, what would it be?
- If you had to change your name, what would you change it to?
- If you woke up tomorrow with no fear, what would you do first?
- If you could send a text message to everyone in the world, what would it say?
- If you could be an animal for a week, what would you be?
- If you could be one age forever, what age would you choose?
- If you could eliminate one class from your day, what would it be?
- If you could have any question answered, what would the question be?
- If you could have one wish that comes true this week, what would it be?
- If you could create a new word that everyone uses, what would it be?

References

Bohanon, Joseph. 2005. "The Talking Circle: A Perspective in Culturally Appropriate Group Work with Indigenous Peoples." http://www.se.edu/nas/files/2013/03/Proceedings-2005-Bohanon.pdf.

Boykin, A. Wade, and Pedro Noguera. 2011. *Creating the Opportunity to Learn: Moving from Research to Practice to Close the Achievement Gap.* Alexandria, VA: Association for Supervision and Curriculum Development (hereafter cited as ASCD).

Boynton, Mark, and Christine Boynton. 2005. *The Educator's Guide to Preventing and Solving Discipline Problems.* Alexandria, VA: ASCD.

CASEL (Collaborative for Academic, Social, and Emotional Learning). 2017. *What Is SEL?* http://www.casel.org/what-is-sel/.

Casteel, Clifton A. 1997. "Attitudes of African American and Caucasian Eighth Grade Students about Praises, Rewards, and Punishments." *Elementary School Guidance and Counseling* 31 (4): 262–72.

Covey, S. R. 2004. *The 7 Habits of Highly Effective People: Restoring the Character Ethic.* Rev. ed. New York: Free Press.

Curtis, Kevin, and Rufus Lott III. 2017. *What Circle Is Not.*

Delpit, Lisa D. 2012. *"Multiplication Is for White People": Raising Expectations for Other People's Children.* New York: New Press.

Finn, J. D. 1989. "Withdrawing from School." *Review of Educational Research* 59: 117–42. http://dx.doi.org/10.3102/00346543059002117.

Fronious, Trevor, Hannah Persson, Sarah Guckenburg, Nancy Hurley, and Anthony Petrosino. 2016. "Restorative Justice in U.S. Schools: A Research Review." https://jprc.wested.org/wp-content/uploads/2016/02/RJ_Literature-Review_20160217.pdf.

Fullan, M. 2001. *Leading in a Culture of Change*. San Francisco: Jossey-Bass.

Hamre, B. K., and R. C. Pianta. 2006. "Student-Teacher Relationships." In *Children's Needs III: Development, Prevention, and Intervention*, edited by G. G. Bear and K. M. Minke, 59–71. Washington, DC: National Association of School Psychologists.

Higgs, C. 2013. *Connecting with Students: Strategies for Building Rapport with Urban Learners*. Lanham, MD: R&L Education.

Jensen, Eric. 2009. *Teaching with Poverty in Mind: What Being Poor Does to Kids' Brains and What Schools Can Do about It*. Alexandria, VA: ASCD.

Kohn, A. 1996. *Beyond Discipline: From Compliance to Community*. Alexandria, VA: ASCD.

Lewin, Roger, and Birute Regine. 2000. *The Soul at Work: Listen . . . Respond . . . Let Go*. New York: Simon & Schuster, 2000. https://www.amazon.com/Soul-Work-Listen-Respond-Let/dp/06848438462.

Living Justice Press. *The Indigenous Origins of Circles and How Non-Natives Learned about Them*. Accessed June 14, 2018. http://www.livingjusticepress.org/index.asp?Type=B_BASIC&SEC=%7B0F6FA816-E094-4B96-8F39-9922F67306E5%7D.

Lopez, Mark. 2009. "Latinos and Education: Explaining the Attainment Gap." http://www.pewhispanic.org/files/reports/115.pdf.

Marzano, R. J., T. Waters, and B. A. McNulty. 2005. *School Leadership That Works: From Research to Results*. Alexandria, VA: ASCD.

Mooney, E. S., and C. A. Thornton. 1999. "Mathematics Attribution Differences by Ethnicity and Socioeconomic Status." *Journal of Education for Students Placed at Risk* 4 (3): 321–32.

References

Morrison, Brenda K., and Dorothy Vaandering. 2012. "Restorative Justice: Pedagogy, Praxis, and Discipline." *Journal of School Violence* 11 (2): 138–55. https://www.researchgate.net/publication/233234044_Restorative_Justice_Pedagogy_Praxis_and_Discipline.

National Education Association (NEA). 2016. *Teaching Children from Poverty and Trauma.* https://www.nea.org/assets/docs/20200_Poverty%20Handbook_flat.pdf.

New York State Office of Children and Family Services. 2016. "Summary Guide for Mandated Reporters in New York State." http://ocfs.ny.gov/main/publications/Pub1159.pdf.

Roorda, D. L. 2012. "Teacher-Child Relationships and Interaction Processes: Effects on Students' Learning Behaviors and Reciprocal Influences between Teacher and Child." Ph.D. diss., University of Amsterdam.

Tatum, Beverly Daniel. 2003. *"Why Are All the Black Kids Sitting Together in the Cafeteria?" and Other Conversations about Race.* New York: Basic Books. https://www.amazon.com/Black-Kids-Sitting-Together-Cafeteria/dp/0465083617.

Umbreit, Mark. 2003. *Talking Circles.* http://www.cehd.umn.edu/ssw/RJP/Projects/Victim-Offender-Dialogue/Peacemaking_Healing_Circles/Talking_Circles.pdf.

U.S. Department of Education. 2016. *REPORT: The State of Racial Diversity in the Educator Workforce.* https://www.ed.gov/news/press-releases/report-state-racial-diversity-educator-workforce.